GEORGE M. COHAN
In His Own Words

Conceived, written and
originally directed by

Chip Deffaa

SAMUEL FRENCH, INC.

45 West 25th Street
NEW YORK 10010
LONDON

7623 Sunset Boulevard
HOLLYWOOD 90046
TORONTO

ALL RIGHTS RESERVED

Copyright © 2002, 2003, 2003, 2004 by Chip Deffaa

CAUTION: Professionals and amateurs are hereby warned that *GEORGE M. COHAN: In His Own Words*, being fully protected under the copyright laws of the United States of America, the British Commonwealth, including Canada, and the other countries of the Copyright Union, is subject to a royalty, and anyone presenting the play without the consent of the owners or their authorized agents will be liable to the penalties by law provided.

Amateurs wishing to arrange for the production of *GEORGE M. COHAN: In His Own Words* must make application to SAMUEL FRENCH, INC., 45 West 25th Street, New York, NY 10010, giving the following particulars:
  (1) The name of the town and theatre or hall in which the proposed production will be presented;
  (2) The maximum seating capacity of the theatre or hall;
  (3) Scale of ticket prices;
  (4) The number of performances intended and the dates thereof.
Upon receipt of these particulars SAMUEL FRENCH, INC. will quote terms and availability.

Stock royalty and availability quoted on application to SAMUEL FRENCH. INC., 45 West 25th Street, New York, NY 10010.

For all other rights than those stipulated above, apply to The Fifi Oscard Agency, 110 W. 40th St., NY, NY 10018 (Attn: Fifi Oscard), (212) 764-1100.

Standard rental package consisting of Piano/Conductor's Score will be loaned two months prior to the production ONLY on receipt of the royalty quoted for all performances, the rental fee and a refundable deposit. The deposit will be refunded on the safe return to SAMUEL FRENCH, INC. of all materials loaned for the production.

Printed in the U.S.A.
0 573 63093 9

No one shall commit or authorize any act or omission by which the copyright of, or the right to copyright, this play may be impaired.

No one shall make any changes in this play for the purpose of production.

Publication of this play does not imply availability for performance. Both amateurs and professionals considering a production are *strongly* advised in their own interests to apply to Samuel French, Inc., for written permission before starting rehearsals, advertising, or booking a theatre.

No part of this book may be reproduced, stored in a retrieval system, or transmitted in any form, by any means, now known or yet to be invented, including mechanical, electronic, photocopying, recording, videotaping, or otherwise, without the prior permission of the publisher.

IMPORTANT BILLING AND CREDIT REQUIREMENTS

All producers of *GEORGE M. COHAN: In His Own Words must* give credit to the Authors of the Work in all programs distributed in connection with performances of the Work, and in all instances in which the title of the Work appears for the purposes of advertising, publicizing or otherwise exploiting a production thereof, including, without limitation, programs, souvenir books and playbills. The names of the Authors must appear on a separate line in which no other matter appears, and *must* be in size of type not less than 50% of the size used for the title of the Work. In addition, the following *must* appear in all programs distributed in connection with performances of the play:

Billing *must* be substantially as follows:

GEORGE M. COHAN
In His Own Words

Conceived, Written and
Originally Directed by

Chip Deffaa

GEORGE M. COHAN: In His Own Words

had its New York premiere at the
Chashama Theater, 135 West 42nd Street,
opening September 11, 2002.

Chip Deffaa conceived, wrote, and directed the production; Sterling Price-McKinney was the musical director/arranger; Justin Boccitto, assistant director/choreographer; Keith Bulla, assistant director. Charlene Gross was the costume designer; Cathy Remmert, stage manager; Jason Brandt, lighting designer; Dawne Swearingen, assistant choreographer/dance captain; Caitlin McLean, assistant stage manager; Stephanie Coburn, lighting operator; Jed Peterson, research assistant; C. Brock, D. W. Barth, production associates; Howard Cruse; graphic designer; Solomon Singer, Scott Stiffler, and Scotti Rhodes, publicists.

The Cast

George M. Cohan	Jon Peterson
Jerry Cohan	Hal Blankenship
Nellie Cohan	Joan Jaffe
Josie Cohan	Dawne Swearingen
Ethel Levey	Suzanne Dressler
Agnes Nolan	Stephanie Saunders
The Reporter, Critic, Erlanger, Keith, etc.	Michael T. Wright
Sam Harris	Erik Schark
Fay Templeton	Jackie Comisar
Male Singer	Daniel Sullivan
Young Actor, Percy, etc	Ellery Bakaitis
Ensemble	Sarah Anders, Sarah Bell, Lauren Blackman, Sandi Hoyt, Anna Reby

Swings: Wendy Porter, Matthew Helton

This production was part of the
Chip Deffaa Invitational Theater Festival
and was made possible with support from Chashama.

This was an Actors' Equity approved Showcase. These actors appeared through the courtesy of Actors Equity: Jon Peterson, Hal Blankenship, Joan Jaffe, Michael T. Wright, Erik Schark, Jackie Comisar, Daniel Sullivan.

A NOTE ABOUT CASTING

In presenting the play, it is recommended that one versatile, middle-aged character actor double as the Reporter ("Ward"), the Male Burlesque Comic, B. F. Keith, A. E. Erlanger, Isidore Witmark, assorted critics, Cohan's doctor and Julian Mitchell. It is recommended that one handsome leading-man type with a good voice double as the Male Singer, Josh Brock, the Distraught Actor and Reporter #1. It is recommended that one youth of about 17 double as the Young Actor ("Chase"), the Young Vaudevillian, Reporter #2 and Percy. Simple changes in costume, voice and attitude should make it clear that these are each distinct characters.

The original New York production used a cast of 16, but if you so choose, you could use more (or fewer) ensemble members (who sing and dance in the bigger musical numbers).

For Zonker

ACT I

A vaudeville-type placard downstage right announces: GEORGE M. COHAN AND HIS ROYAL FAMILY. The stand holding this placard is pre-set with three different hand-lettered placards already in place. The top placard—which we see at the start of the play—says "George M. Cohan and His Royal Family;" the next placard, underneath it, says, "The Four Cohans;" the next placard says "Mr. Cohan, Alone"—so that at later points in the play, the top-most placard can be removed and carried offstage, revealing the next placard.

This play is designed to be mounted in a minimalist fashion, with little in terms of sets and props; the audience's imagination will fill in the rest.

There is a coatrack, with an overcoat and fedora, at stage right and a folding screen draped with red, white and blue bunting at stage left.

We are seeing the stage for a show in rehearsal with standard black curtains ("legs") in the wings. Two rolling black panels are positioned upstage, angled to jut out a bit in front of a black rear curtain or a black rolling panel to provide two additional upstage points of entry and exit—referred to hereafter as the upstage left slot and the upstage right slot.

The director has great flexibility in deciding exactly where/when characters will enter and exit and move. In the first New York production of this show, characters sometimes entered from one side of the audience or the other onto the stage or exited from one side of the stage and then walked around in back of the audience to make their next entrance from the other side. But what is practical in one theater may not be practical in another theater configured differently. The main thing is that characters seen in brief vignettes are brought on and off quickly—and from different points for variety's sake—maintaining the flow of the play. Cohan's plays moved swiftly; that tradition should be represented.

A sole piano will suffice for musical accompaniment. The piano is positioned downstage right (if desired, a little alcove can be created with black curtains to help separate the piano, coatrack, and vaudeville placards from the main performance area of the stage); atop the piano are pieces of sheet music and a newspaper—props which may be utilized later. If this show is performed on a stage that is very small the piano may be positioned in the wings instead of onstage. The show incorporates twenty-six Cohan songs written between 1897 and 1922. In the tradition of the time, virtually all songs—except when Cohan is singing to his wife—are played directly to the audience rather than to other characters onstage.

(The house lights go down. The music begins, then lights come up as COHAN, in military costume, bounds on stage—entering from upstage right slot—and performs with great panache the song "YOU'RE A GRAND OLD FLAG.")

GEORGE M. COHAN. *(Sings, brightly:)*
THERE'S A FEELING COMES A-STEALING
AND IT SETS MY BRAIN TO REELING,
WHEN I'M LIST'NING TO THE MUSIC OF A MILITARY BAND.
ANY TUNE LIKE "YANKEE DOODLE"
SIMPLY SETS ME OFF MY NOODLE.
IT'S THAT PATRIOTIC SOMETHING
THAT NO ONE CAN UNDERSTAND.
"WAY DOWN SOUTH IN THE LAND OF COTTON ..."
MELODY UNTIRING,
AIN'T THAT INSPIRING.
HURRAH! HURRAH! WE'LL JOIN THE JUBILEE.
AND THAT'S GOING SOME
FOR THE YANKEES, BY GUM!
RED, WHITE AND BLUE,
I AM FOR YOU.
HONEST, YOU'RE A GRAND OLD FLAG.

YOU'RE A GRAND OLD FLAG,
YOU'RE A HIGH-FLYING FLAG.
AND FOREVER IN PEACE MAY YOU WAVE.
YOU'RE THE EMBLEM OF
THE LAND I LOVE,
THE HOME OF THE FREE AND THE BRAVE.
EV'RY HEART BEATS TRUE

UNDER RED, WHITE AND BLUE.
WHERE THERE'S NEVER A BOAST OR BRAG.
"BUT SHOULD AULD ACQUAINTANCE BE FORGOT."
KEEP YOUR EYE ON THE GRAND OLD FLAG.

I'M NO CRANKY, HANKY PANKY,
I'M A DEAD SQUARE HONEST YANKEE.
AND I'M MIGHTY PROUD OF THAT OLD FLAG
THAT FLIES FOR UNCLE SAM.
THOUGH I DON'T BELIEVE IN RAVING,
EVERY TIME I SEE IT WAVING,
THERE'S A CHILL RUNS UP MY BACK
THAT MAKES ME GLAD I'M WHAT I AM.

HERE'S A LAND WITH A MILLION SOLDIERS,
THAT'S IF WE SHOULD NEED 'EM.
WE'LL FIGHT FOR FREEDOM!
HURRAH! HURRAH! FOR EV'RY YANKEE TAR
AND OLD G.A.R.,
EV'RY STRIPE, EV'RY STAR.
RED, WHITE AND BLUE,
HATS OFF TO YOU.
HONEST, YOU'RE A GRAND OLD FLAG.

YOU'RE A GRAND OLD FLAG,
YOU'RE A HIGH-FLYING FLAG.
AND FOREVER IN PEACE MAY YOU WAVE.
YOU'RE THE EMBLEM OF
THE LAND I LOVE,
THE HOME OF THE FREE AND THE BRAVE.
EV'RY HEART BEATS TRUE
UNDER RED, WHITE AND BLUE.
WHERE THERE'S NEVER A BOAST OR BRAG.
"BUT SHOULD AULD ACQUAINTANCE BE FORGOT,
SHOULD AULD ACQUAINTANCE BE FORGOT,
SHOULD AULD ACQUAINTANCE BE FORGOT,"
KEEP YOUR EYE ON THE GRAND OLD FLAG.

GEORGE M. COHAN. *(Hereafter identified as GMC, speaking to the audience.)* Give your show a strong opening number and you're halfway home.

(A YOUNG ACTOR enters from the wings stage right.)

YOUNG ACTOR. But Mr. Cohan, we open in two weeks, and you still haven't given us the show's second act yet.
GMC. Tell me what you'd like to wear in the second act, and maybe you'll give me an idea of what to write for a second act. Relax, Chase. No Cohan show has yet opened with the second act unwritten—although there've been a few times when I wrote it within forty-eight hours of opening night.

(YOUNG ACTOR exits.
JERRY COHAN enters from wings stage right.)

JERRY COHAN. It's gonna be a great show, son.

(NELLIE COHAN and JOSIE COHAN enter from upstage left, trailed by a REPORTER.)

NELLIE COHAN. George....
GMC. Yes, mother.
NELLIE. A gentleman from the press is here to see you.

(GMC steps behind a folding screen draped with patriotic bunting to change from the military costume into a dapper suit. His father, mother and sister remain present as the reporter—played by the same actor who will also later double as critics, producers, and a song publisher—attempts to interview him.)

REPORTER. What is your new show about, Mr. Cohan?
GMC. *(While changing his costume behind the screen and popping his head out to speak as needed.)* "The Yankee Prince" will be even bigger, brighter, more colorful, and more patriotic than my current hit, "George Washington Jr." *(Gesturing as he speaks to introduce family members, who acknowledge his references to them.)* My father is in it, my mother is in it, my sister is in it, and I'm in it. This may be the last time you'll see the Four Cohans on the stage. We've been together thirty years. You know, Mom and Pop took me on the road with them and my sister as soon as I was born.
REPORTER. The billing reads, "George M. Cohan and His Royal Family."
JERRY. That should be: "George M. Cohan and his family

royalties."

JOSIE COHAN. *(Teasingly, playfully crossing to GMC.)* Oh, Mr. Cohan, can you write a play without a flag in it?

GMC. I can write a play without anything but a pencil.

REPORTER. Your love of country is well known.

GMC. I love the *ideals* of this country—which our politicians don't often live up to.

REPORTER. But what exactly is your new show *about*?

GMC. Oh, you know I never like to give too much away before the opening, Ward. But confidentially, there's a leading man and a leading lady.... And in the Second Act, when he's very angry at her, he reads Ibsen to her.

(JOSIE COHAN helps GMC—who is out from behind the screen—as he finishes dressing, straightening his collar or adjusting his tie; they are close and she is clearly used to helping him.)

REPORTER. You don't like Ibsen?

GMC. Actually I admire him very much. But we work a bit differently. My goal is to entertain the public.

NELLIE. On what lines have you usually constructed your plays?

GMC. Mostly on the Pennsylvania and New York Central.

REPORTER. You're the most successful playwright in the country right now—

GMC. *(Crossing to the REPORTER.)* And songwriter. And actor. And singer.

REPORTER. Have you a theory of popular playwriting?

GMC. First, think of something to say. Then say it the way the theatergoer wants to hear it said—meaning you must lie like the Dickens.

JOSIE. George, you're not really answering the gentleman's questions.

GMC. To quote a bit from my new play: "What does it matter who I am, as long as I amuse you? ... I just love the drama of it all." *(Crosses to downstage right.)* Speaking on the square, now.... After I finish writing one act, I haven't any more idea than you have what the next act will be. I write my plays after midnight. I get back to my apartment after the theater and have supper—a big one, too: a pound of beefsteak, a large collection of fried potatoes and a pot of coffee. Then I write steadily until nine in the morning. Get some rest, and then do the next show. You have to write what you know. For me, that often turns out to be Broadway. No one's ever loved her more.

REPORTER. Broadway? A street?
GMC. Sure, it's the greatest street in the world.
JERRY. Some people say it's terrible.
GMC. Philadelphia people.

(GMC crosses up to his parents.)

NELLIE. And some say it's wonderful.
GMC. That's just it. It's terribly wonderful.
REPORTER. I don't understand.
GMC. Nobody understands Broadway. People hate it and don't know why. People love it and don't know why. It's just because it's Broadway.
REPORTER. That's a mystery, isn't it?
GMC. That's what it is, a mystery. And I've always savored mysteries.

(The REPORTER, NELLIE COHAN, JOSIE COHAN and JERRY COHAN exit—carrying the folding screen offstage with them—leaving GMC alone on stage. He moves to downstage center. Lights shift.)

GMC. *(To audience.)* In my time, I owned Broadway. I don't just mean I owned theaters. Though I certainly owned some of them. My flagship theater—the George M. Cohan Theater—stood on this very block. So if you're seeking to commune with the spirit of George M. Cohan, you've come to the right neighborhood. I starred in shows all around here—at the Henry Miller Theater, on the next block; and at the Hudson Theater, another block over. Some of my greatest triumphs occurred right on this street: "Little Johnny Jones" at the Liberty Theater on 42nd Street, "45 Minutes from Broadway" just down the street at the New Amsterdam Theater.

This was my world. I worked on Broadway, and on the road, in theaters like this. In the first decades of the twentieth century, I dominated American theater in a way that no other man ever has, before or since. And I relished my position.

(Song: "THE MAN WHO OWNS BROADWAY." From the top of the

piano GMC picks up a newspaper, which he uses as a prop in this number, since the lyrics refer to the papers saying he is the man who owns Broadway. GMC sings the verse and one chorus by himself, alone on the stage. Then 10 MEMBERS OF THE ENSEMBLE—virtually everyone except his family—come out on stage, entering from upstage left and left slot, to sing and dance behind GMC, carrying newspapers as if reading about him. They sing a chorus of the song—in a somewhat hushed, staccato manner—while providing a moving backdrop for GMC as he tap dances throughout the second chorus.)

GMC. *(Sings:)*
THE MAN WHO BROKE THE BANK AT MONTE CARLO IS A JOKE,
THE MAN WHO BROKE THE BROKERS IS A DEAD ONE FOR HE'S BROKE.
AND OTHERS WHOM YOU'VE HEARD OF AND HAVE SUNG OF IN YOUR DAY,
HAVE ALL PASSED ON THEIR WAY,
THEY WERE NOT HERE TO STAY.
BUT CAST YOUR OPTICS ON A MAN WHO'S ALL THE MONEY,
ALL THE HONEY,
PRIDE OF THE TOWN,
TALK OF NEW YORK.
YOU'D SWEAR I'D WON THE CHAMPIONSHIP
OR FOUND THE GREAT NORTH POLE.
THE STREETS ARE ALL BLOCKADED EV'RY TIME I TAKE A STROLL.
THE STARING CROWDS AMASS
AND MURMUR AS I PASS ...

HE IS THE MAN WHO OWNS BROADWAY,
THAT'S WHAT THE DAILY PAPERS SAY.
THE GIRLS ARE TURNED AWAY
AT EV'RY MATINEE.
THEY GO TO SEE THE PLAYER NOT THE PLAY, THEY SAY.
KINGS ON THEIR THRONE MAY ENVIOUS BE,
HE'S GOT THE POPULARITY.
IF THERE'S ANYTHING IN NEW YORK THAT YOU SEE YOU WANT JUST SAY.

DROP A LINE OR WIRE
TO THE SOLE PROPRIETOR,
THE MAN WHO OWNS BROADWAY.
THEY SAY HE IS THE MAN WHO OWNS BROADWAY.

MEMBERS OF THE ENSEMBLE. *(Sing in somewhat hushed voices:)*
HE IS THE MAN WHO OWNS BROADWAY,
THAT'S WHAT THE DAILY PAPERS SAY.
THE GIRLS ARE TURNED AWAY
AT EV'RY MATINEE.
THEY GO TO SEE THE PLAYER NOT THE PLAY, THEY SAY.
KINGS ON THEIR THRONE MAY ENVIOUS BE,
HE'S GOT THE POPULARITY.

IF THERE'S ANYTHING IN NEW YORK THAT YOU SEE YOU
    WANT JUST SAY.
DROP A LINE OR WIRE
TO THE SOLE PROPRIETOR,
THE MAN WHO OWNS BROADWAY.
THEY SAY HE IS THE MAN WHO OWNS BROADWAY.

(Everyone except GMC exits. They exit upstage left. GMC crosses to downstage right. He puts the newspaper back down on the piano.)

GMC. *(To audience.)* I guess Broadway, for me, was everything in life I've never had: my education, and the friendship, games, adventures, and just plain fun of boyhood and growing up.

(GMC exits into wings stage right. He removes his suit jacket. He does not wear his suit jacket for the scenes set in his boyhood. Blackout. Lights come up. The YOUNG ACTOR changes the vaudeville placard at stage right; he removes the top placard and carries it offstage, so that we now see a placard announcing: "The Four Cohans."
SONG: The Four Cohans harmonize on "I WAS BORN IN VIRGINIA." The number starts off with just JERRY and NELLIE coming on stage from the upstage right slot, showing how the act began with the parents before their children were part of it. After singing the verse and a chorus, the parents go back into the

wings at stage right, as if the song were ending, but then re-emerge for another chorus—this time trailed by their children, GEORGE and JOSIE, who join them to sing one chorus all together.)

JERRY. *(Sings:)*
I WAS BORN IN A SOUTHERN STATE, WHERE ALL
 NATURE'S SUBLIME,
NELLIE. *(Sings:)*
IN A CITY WHERE THE GALS ARE PRETTY, AND THE SUN
 SHINES NEARLY ALL THE TIME.
JERRY. *(Sings:)*
HOSPITALITY THERE YOU'LL FIND,
NELLIE. *(Sings:)*
BRIGHT SMILES EV'RY WHERE.

JERRY and NELLIE. *(Sing:)*
WHEN I LOOK 'ROUN' AND SEE SOME OTHER TOWN,
I'M MIGHTY GLAD I COME FROM THERE ...
I WAS BORN IN VIRGINIA,
THAT'S THE STATE THAT WILL WIN YER.
IF YOU'VE GOT A SOUL IN YER,
AIN'T NO SOUTHERN FROWN.
IN THE CITY OF NORFOLK,
HOME OF BEAUTIES AND WAR TALK,
RECKON YOU'LL LIKE IT,
IF YOU SHOULD STRIKE IT,
THAT DOGGARN TOWN.

(JERRY and NELLIE strut off into the wings stage right as they finish singing the chorus above; they come out of the wings again, with their children following them, to continue singing. The music is raised a half step for this second chorus, to create a feeling of added brightness.)

JERRY, NELLIE, JOSIE and GMC. *(Sing:)*
I WAS BORN IN VIRGINIA,
THAT'S THE STATE THAT WILL WIN YER.
IF YOU'VE GOT A SOUL IN YER,
AIN'T NO SOUTHERN FROWN.
IN THE CITY OF NORFOLK,

HOME OF BEAUTIES AND WAR TALK,
RECKON YOU'LL LIKE IT,
IF YOU SHOULD STRIKE IT,
THAT DOGGARN TOWN.

(All exit into wings stage right as they finish the song. GMC re-emerges to give his curtain speech, standing center stage; the family members enter and exit as he mentions them.)

GMC. *(Curtain speech, to audience.)* My father thanks you, my mother thanks you, my sister thanks you, and I thank you. *(Moves to a position more towards stage left. To audience.)*

Actually, I was born in Providence, Rhode Island, in 1878—on the Fourth of July. As a boy, I thought all those celebrations—the fireworks, the flag-waving—were in honor of my birthday. But there was something about my sharing my birthday with my nation that got to me. I often had flags and patriotic bunting in my shows—not just on the stage but in my own dressing rooms.

The great loves in my life were family—my mother, my father and my sister. And the theater—the only world I ever really knew or felt comfortable in. And my country.

(NELLIE and JERRY enter from wings stage right.)

NELLIE. *(To audience.)* People used to ask why I took on the trouble of carrying Josie and George as infants around with us. Why, they weren't any bother at all. They could be parked in a trunk or a dresser drawer. Those made fine beds.

JERRY. *(To audience.)* We were wandering minstrels—and so penniless it was a joke. Sometimes Mrs. Cohan and I had to walk for miles, carrying the children in our arms to the theater, because we didn't have money for streetcar fare. But I always knew the good times were just ahead.

NELLIE. *(To audience.)* I carried George on stage with us for the first time when he was four months old, and that tiny baby loved it, I could tell. It felt good for him to be there. The stage, after all, is a place of love.

GMC. *(To audience.)* I never had a formal education.

NELLIE. *(To audience.)* He had a total of six weeks in public school—Providence's E Street School—when he was eight.

GMC. *(To audience.)* I was a highly active child. The principal advised my parents that they could calm me down by serving me a bit of the painkiller laudanum—that's a solution of opium in alcohol. My parents, however, did not believe I needed to be medicated—I needed to be performing.

My father and mother, and my sister Josie, taught me the show business: singing, dancing, how to hold a stage, and the rudiments of music.

(NELLIE bows to JERRY, who sings gently—either a capella or with piano accompaniment—the first lines of the chorus of the song "ALWAYS LEAVE THEM LAUGHING WHEN YOU SAY GOODBYE," suggesting a bit of a soft shoe and adding a flourish with a cane.)

JERRY. *(Sings:)*
ALWAYS LEAVE THEM LAUGHING WHEN YOU SAY
   GOODBYE.
NEVER LINGER LONG ABOUT
OR ELSE YOU'LL WEAR YOUR WELCOME OUT.
WHEN YOU MEET A FELLOW WITH A TEAR-DIMMED EYE,
YOU CAN LEAVE HIM LAUGHING IF YOU TRY....

(JOSIE enters from downstage left, takes her place near GMC.)

NELLIE. *(To audience.)* I never saw a brother and sister closer than young George and Josie. Two best pals. And both delighted in mimicking their parents. I loved the time when we had them in the act as dancing dolls—little wooden dolls who came to life at night.

(Song: GMC and JOSIE bow to one another and dance in place a bit to the melody of "ALWAYS LEAVE THEM LAUGHING WHEN YOU SAY GOODBYE" as heard above. The pianist should suggest a music-box feel. The dancing of GMC and JOSIE here should be jerky, marionette-like, but also evoke the movements we have seen their parents make so we see that they've learned from watching their parents. They can simply dance to the melody of this song or, if desired, they can also sing the lyrics which JERRY just sang.)

GMC. *(To audience.)* I can't remember a day when I wasn't working with my family. I can't remember a day—whether as a child or an adult—when my father didn't greet me with a kiss.

JERRY. *(Crosses to GMC, kisses him, and tells audience:)* I recorded in my diary that George wrote his first song, and proudly tried it out on me, when he was just four years old. The entire lyrics, which I preserved in that diary, were: "Damn it to hell. *Damn* it to hell. Damn it to hell. *Damn* it hell...."

(JERRY crosses back to stand by NELLIE.)

GMC. *(To audience.)* I can't remember ever wanting to be any place other than the theater.

JERRY. *(To audience.)* Well, I did note in my diary that there were a few times, when George was very young, when he'd look out the window of whatever boarding house we were staying in that week, and cry because he'd see other children playing. And he had to stay inside, practicing his violin or a dance step. But he very quickly came to love the theater just as deeply as I did. And he was always learning.

GMC. *(To audience.)* I saw the country—the theaters of the country, anyway. And learned the important facts about each city—at least the facts that mattered most to one growing up in the show business. I learned my ABC's.... As I wrote:

"A stands for Albany, good for one night.

B stands for Boston, for two weeks all right.

C for Chicago, big money, no yaps.

D stands for Denver, break even perhaps ...."

Well, you get the idea....

When you're living out of a trunk—when home is a succession of hotels and boarding houses, in one strange city after another, when you don't have schoolmates to pal around with—your family becomes your only constant. Your only security in a hard world.

NELLIE. *(To audience.)* We four were sufficient unto each other.

JERRY. *(To audience.)* And it wouldn't have been wise to let George grow too attached to children in cities we visited. Not when we'd be leaving soon and he'd never see those children again.

NELLIE. *(To audience.)* George was a great one for observing people. If we got to a new city, he could amuse himself simply by going downtown and watching passersby. Later, he'd imitate for us the way people he'd seen had walked and talked.

JERRY. *(To audience.)* As our act did better and we began making a little money, I'd give George an allowance. He'd put some

coins in one pocket, and some in the other.
   GMC. *(To audience.)* I liked to feel my pockets were filled with money.
   JERRY. *(To audience.)* Then he'd go downtown and give it all away. Maybe buy ice cream for some children. Maybe offer some coins to older people who looked poor. I'd never discourage kindness. Especially in a child who worked so hard.
   GMC. I was ten when I wrote what I remember as my first actual song. The chorus went:
"There's Kate and Nancy
Billy, Clancy, Dan and Mike Magee.
There's Pat O'Day and Hughie Fay,
All loaded down with glee
There's Jimmy Grogan, Johnny Logan,
Both so big and blimp,
At number three the boulevard,
The first floor front."

(JERRY crosses over to GMC.)

   JERRY. *(Gives GEORGE a kiss on forehead and says:)* We'll be sending your songs out to publishers soon.
   GMC. *(To audience.)* I remember the first letter I got back from an honest-to-God New York song publisher: "Dear Sir: Your songs are not publishable. Please do not send us any more." For a lad of eleven, though, it was nice being called "sir."
   JERRY. *(To GMC.)* Don't worry about publishers, son. If you write songs that are good enough, we'll use them in the family act.
   GMC. *(To audience.)* I wrote a song or two a week. I loved writing for my family. Especially Josie. I always told her she inspired some of my very best work.

(JOSIE smiles in acknowledgment; GMC and JOSIE exit, leaving the parents on stage.
Song: "OH, YOU WONDERFUL GIRL." The parents sing the first chorus. Then JOSIE comes onstage, followed by GMC. She dances about as GMC sings the second chorus to her as if he were a suitor.)

   JERRY and NELLIE. *(Sing:)*
OH YOU WONDERFUL GIRL,

WHAT A WONDERFUL GIRL YOU ARE.
YOU'VE MADE THE WORLD APPEAR TO ME,
NEAR TO ME,
DEAR TO ME;
OH THOSE WONDERFUL EYES
THRILL ME THROUGH.
IT SEEMS TO ME
TO BE A WONDERFUL WORLD,
SINCE I MET YOU.

(JOSIE enters, followed by GMC. She dances about as GMC sings to her. She fits little, high-pitched vocal obligatoes—singing the syllables "ah-ah"—into the rests on his third, fourth and fifth lines.)

GMC. *(Sings:)*
OH YOU WONDERFUL GIRL,
WHAT A WONDERFUL GIRL YOU ARE.
YOU'VE MADE THE WORLD APPEAR TO ME,
    JOSIE. *(Sings:)*
AH-AH.
    GMC. *(Sings:)*
NEAR TO ME,
    JOSIE. *(Sings:)*
AH-AH.
    GMC. *(Sings:)*
DEAR TO ME.
    JOSIE. *(Sings:)*
AH-AH.

GMC and JOSIE. *(Sing to each other:)*
OH THOSE WONDERFUL EYES
THRILL ME THROUGH.
IT SEEMS TO ME
TO BE A WONDERFUL WORLD,
SINCE I MET YOU.

(GMC and JOSIE exit into wings stage right.)

NELLIE. *(To audience.)* Soon George wasn't just writing songs and gags for us, he was pressing his material on half the performers we met.

JERRY. *(To audience.)* George was filled with talent. And filled with personality. Everyone was saying that.

NELLIE. *(To audience.)* Well, actually some were saying a bit more than that.... Mr. Cohan and I may not have been the greatest of disciplinarians.

(JOSIE enters from upstage right.)

JOSIE. *(To audience.)* George could seem a bit fresh, to some.

NELLIE. *(To audience.)* He could, in plain English, be a handful. We had family friends, the Higginsons, in Orange, New Jersey, who kindly offered to take George in for a season. Let him have a taste of a normal, healthy American boyhood in a small town, growing up around other children. Fresh air, sunshine, baseball, church, discipline, chores....

JERRY. *(To audience.)* The experiment did not last long.

NELLIE. *(To audience.)* The Higginsons quickly returned George to us by train. *(GMC enters from downstage left.)* I told him *(Speaking to GMC.)* I hope you weren't too much for our friends.

GMC. *(To his mother.)* Now don't you worry one bit. Mom and Pop ... Mr. Higginson told me to assure you that he still thinks just as much of the both of you, and of Josie, as ever.

JERRY. *(To audience.)* I tried to have one of the really good musicians I knew give George proper training on the violin.

GMC. *(To audience.)* But within two weeks, that man gave me a note to take home to my father: "It is impossible to teach this boy anything. He knows it all...."

JERRY. *(To audience.)* George just needed the right outlet for his energy. He thrived the year we toured doing the comedy "Peck's Bad Boy," with George in the title role.

GMC. *(To audience.)* That was when I first showed everybody I could *act*. I was 13. And boy, I knew—old Edwin Booth had nothing on me!

JOSIE. *(To audience.)* George portrayed, the program said, an "incorrigible lad with a heart of gold." In the play, he had to raise Cain from start to finish. His acting was *very* convincing.

GMC. *(To audience, pantomiming the action he describes, with his sister, father and mother playing the others he mentions.)* As "Peck's Bad Boy," I got to cheerfully throw one girl out the window, toss coal into the face of my dear old Pa, push a police officer into a washtub filled with soapsuds—and boast: "I can lick any kid in town!"

JOSIE. *(To audience.)* Of course, there were kids at the stage door of theaters across the country waiting to take slugs at him after the show.

GMC. *(To audience.)* When we played the Opera House in Poughkeepsie, New York, some kids actually threw stones at me. And rotten potatoes!

JERRY. *(To GMC.)* Don't let it get to you, son. Don't let it get to you.

GMC. *(To audience.)* I didn't. But for the rest of my life, I never performed again in Poughkeepsie.

JOSIE. *(To audience.)* I admired George so much. I knew he'd make it big someday. I used to wonder if he'd make it as an actor or a playwright or a singer or a dancer or a songwriter; he loved it all.

GMC. *(To audience.)* Some songwriter! I was 14 years old, and still unpublished. That rankled me.

JOSIE. *(To audience.)* That summer we stayed such a long time in Providence, Rhode Island, we almost began to put down roots. Some of the local kids even invited George to play baseball, but he never could throw a ball too well.

GMC. *(To JOSIE.)* When was I supposed to have learned how to pitch? And I bet none of those boys knew how to do a decent buck-and-wing.

(JOSIE, JERRY and NELLIE exit.)

GMC. *(To audience.)* That summer, I got close to a musician in the orchestra, Josh Brock. *(BROCK enters from downstage left, looks at GMC admiringly. He should stand close enough to GMC to be able to pat him on the shoulder or back, or make some kind of contact, when he addresses GMC.)* The first grown man to ever treat me like an equal. When I wasn't performing, you'd find me sitting by him in the orchestra pit. All the other musicians became my friends, too. But Josh was something else. He'd take me swimming. Anything I had to say was of interest to him. I'd try out songs on him.

JOSH. *(To GMC.)* You've got the goods. I tell all the other musicians: That young George M. is a genius.

GMC. *(To JOSH.)* I wish the publishers felt that way. I've mailed my songs to every firm—no luck.

JOSH. *(To GMC.)* Anything you want in life, you *ask* for it.

Personally. Don't just mail your songs to the publishers. Next time you're in New York, march right in to the office of Witmark. George, when you want to, you can charm the pants off anyone. Let 'em see that handsome Irish mug. Let 'em feel your determination. You're going to be in this business a long time. Make 'em listen to you!

GMC. *(To audience.)* That Josh Brock gave me confidence. *(BROCK exits upstage left.)* Youth needs confidence.

On September 5th, the day our family arrived in New York for a two-week booking, I marched into the offices of Witmark, the biggest of publishers. *(WITMARK enters from downstage left.)* Isidore Witmark told me:

ISIDORE WITMARK. *(To GMC.)* My family's been enjoying your family in variety shows for years.

GMC. Well, Mr. Witmark, I've written a peppy number you're gonna love— "Why Did Nellie Leave Her Home?"

(GMC shows WITMARK a song he's been carrying in his pocket.)

ISIDORE WITMARK. *(Looking the song over.)* That title's got something..... Say, young man, out of respect for your family I'll buy this song of yours outright. I can pay $10.

GMC. I'll never forget this day, Mr. Witmark. And when I can, I'll return the favor. I'm going to be in this business a long time. Someday you'll come to me for something. And out of respect for you, I'll help *you* out. I'll treat you just the way you're treating me today, Mr. Witmark. Because that's the kind of a little guy I am.

(WITMARK exits, upstage left.)

GMC. *(To audience.)* I couldn't wait for my song to be published. That week, there was another family act on the vaudeville bill. I asked the youngest member of that act if he'd like to introduce my new song to the world. *(A YOUNG VAUDEVILLE PERFORMER enters from upstage right; he crosses down towards GMC; he'd obviously just as soon keep moving, if GMC weren't stopping him. To YOUNG VAUDEVILLE PERFORMER, while trying to hand him some music.)* You could learn it now, sing it on stage tonight.

YOUNG VAUDEVILLIAN. *(Holding up a pouch of tobacco or a cigarette.)* I was just going out for a smoke.

GMC. You could learn it tomorrow, on your day off, sing it Tuesday.

YOUNG VAUDEVILLIAN. I got relatives to visit, in Brooklyn.

GMC. Don't you think about theater on your day off? I never think about anything *but* the theater.

YOUNG VAUDEVILLIAN. But we've already got a good act; why change it? Everyone knows—if you've got a good vaudeville act, you've got security for life.

GMC. Listen! Just look at this song. I'm telling you, I've got the goods.

YOUNG VAUDEVILLIAN. *(Reading the music GMC has given him.)* "Why Did Nellie Leave Her Home?"

GMC. Izzy Witmark is crazy about that title. See, I picked the name "Nellie" because that's my mother's name. I've got the greatest mother. And everything about mothers is usually all right, you know?... The song came to me in a flash. I overheard my mother telling a woman about some poor young gal who *had* to leave home. I couldn't imagine why anyone would leave a home—I mean, if they were lucky enough to have a home.

YOUNG VAUDEVILLIAN. I'll explain it to you later.

GMC. Just learn this song! Once it's published, the whole city will be singing my words. *(To audience.)* But that's not exactly the way it worked out.

YOUNG VAUDEVILLIAN. *(To GMC.)* Hey, Cohan! Today Witmark published "Why Did Nellie Leave Her Home?" And it's nothing like that song you claimed to have written.

GMC. *(To audience.)* Isidore Witmark had bought my song, all right! He kept the title. But he got some writer to create all different lyrics, and turn my comic number into a weepy ballad. I was humiliated!

But I still had my ambition. When our family had a week-long layoff, I told the theater owner I'd perform solo, and at week's end he could pay me whatever he felt I deserved.

(Lights shift.)

GMC. *(To YOUNG VAUDEVILLIAN.)* Can you beat that? I told him to pay me whatever I was worth—and he handed me *six bucks*.

YOUNG VAUDEVILLIAN. What's the extra buck for?

(YOUNG VAUDEVILLIAN exits, downstage left.)

GMC. *(To audience.)* At least my family appreciated me. *(JOSIE* *enters from upstage left slot. She crosses down to GMC.)* For the next couple of years, I wrote material for them furiously.

JOSIE. *(To GMC.)* I'll always sing your songs, George.

GMC. *(To audience.)* Josie was my biggest booster. *(To JOSIE.)* Did we ever quarrel?

JOSIE. *(To GMC.)* Only when you spent too much time in the tub. *(To audience.)* My brother liked to take three baths a day!

GMC. *(To audience.)* A lifelong habit. I got some of my best ideas soaking in the tub.

Oh, everybody loved Josie. She was so pretty! I had to work to keep the guys away from her! And she was the most talented gal I knew! I gave her my best material. Promised her I always would.

JOSIE. *(To audience.)* But I'd tell anyone who asked: George is going to be the real star. And he wants it the most.

GMC. *(To audience.)* Josie turned down countless offers to go solo. She would have been content just touring the country with us in vaudeville, all her life.

(NELLIE enters from upstage left slot.)

NELLIE COHAN. *(To audience.)* We *all* would have been content with that. It was a good life.

GMC. *(To audience.)* But my goal was Broadway. My songs were developing rapidly now. And I was emerging as the focus of our family's act.

(JERRY enters from upstage right slot to join the family for the next song. He is carrying two bouquets for use in the next song, one of which he now hands off to GMC. During the song, GMC will presents his bouquet to JOSIE, JERRY will present his bouquet to NELLIE. Song: GMC and the family perform "YOU REMIND ME OF MY MOTHER.")

GMC. *(Sings to JOSIE:)*
YOU REMIND ME OF MY MOTHER.
MY MOTHER WAS A LOT LIKE YOU.
SO MANY LITTLE THINGS YOU DO,
I FIND THEY BRING TO MIND MY MOTHER.
JERRY. *(Sings to NELLIE:)*
I NEVER THOUGHT THERE'D BE ANOTHER
WOULD HAVE THAT SWEET APPEAL,

OR COULD MAKE ME FEEL
THAT THE OLD FOOL WORLD WAS REAL.
    GMC. *(Sings to JOSIE:)*
I'VE GOT A TINTYPE OF MY MOTHER
WHEN MOTHER WAS A GIRL LIKE YOU.
YOU LOOK A LOT ALIKE, YOU TWO.
HER HAIR WAS JUST AS FAIR.
    JERRY. *(Sings to NELLIE:)*
HER EYES USED TO TWINKLE JUST THE SAME AS YOUR
    EYES DO.
    GMC and JERRY. *(Sing to JOSIE and NELLIE:)*
YOU REMIND ME OF MY MOTHER.
THAT'S WHY I LOVE YOU.

(The music of the chorus begins again. We hear just the piano for the first four lines while the Cohans dance about a bit. Then NELLIE and JOSIE take up the song.)

    JOSIE and NELLIE. *(Sing to GMC and JERRY:)*
YOU NEVER THOUGHT THERE'D BE ANOTHER
WOULD HAVE THAT SWEET APPEAL,
OR COULD MAKE YOU FEEL
THAT THE OLD FOOL WORLD WAS REAL.
    GMC and JERRY. *(Sing—JOSIE and NELLIE can, if desired, hum behind them, as indicated in the score.)*
I'VE GOT A TINTYPE OF MY MOTHER
WHEN MOTHER WAS A GIRL LIKE YOU.
YOU LOOK A LOT ALIKE, YOU TWO.
HER HAIR WAS JUST AS FAIR.
HER EYES USED TO TWINKLE JUST THE SAME AS YOUR
    EYES DO.
YOU REMIND ME OF MY MOTHER.
THAT'S WHY I LOVE YOU.

(This number segues right into the next. When the family finishes singing "You Remind Me of My Mother" there is a bit of play-off music to accompany the family as they exit into the stage-right wings. GMC quickly bounds back on stage by himself to go right into the next song. He sings, very brightly, one chorus of "I GUESS I'LL HAVE TO TELEGRAPH MY BABY.")

GMC. *(Sings:)*
WELL I GUESS I'LL HAVE TO TELEGRAPH MY BABY,
I NEED THE MONEY BAD,
INDEED I DO.
FOR LUCY IS A VERY GEN'ROUS LADY,
I CAN ALWAYS TOUCH HER FOR A FEW.
I FIND THE WESTERN UNION A CONVENIENCE,
NO MATTER WHERE I ROAM.
I'LL TELEGRAPH MY BABY,
SHE'LL SEND TEN OR TWENTY MAYBE.
THEN I WON'T HAVE TO WALK BACK HOME.
OH YES, OH YES, I'LL TELEGRAPH FOR PLENTY,
ASK FOR TEN BUT SHE'LL SEND TWENTY,
WON'T HAVE TO WALK BACK HOME.

(NELLIE enters from upstage left slot.)

NELLIE COHAN. *(To audience.)* I thought it amazing he could write such ditties. I figured he was too young to even know what the term "baby" meant in songs like that.

GMC. *(To audience.)* Oh, I had some idea. Even Pop realized that when, at age fifteen, I ran away. I tried to elope with a gal I'd met—a fellow performer a bit older than me. Pop had a detective track me down and bring me back.

(JERRY COHAN enters from upstage left slot.)

JERRY COHAN. Concentrate on the act!

(JOSIE COHAN enters from upstage left slot.
Song excerpt: "I WANT YOU." GMC hands sheet music to the rest of his family, starts singing the song alone—as if teaching them a new song he's just written—and they join in. GMC can pick up the sheet music from the piano to give it out to his family. Or it could be carried onstage by family members.)

GMC. *(Sings:)*
I WANT YOU,
YES I DO.
YOU, JUST YOU, YOU.

GMC, JOSIE, JERRY and NELLIE. *(Sing:)*
CAN'T YOU UNDERSTAND ME?
I DON'T CARE ABOUT
THE PRESENTS THAT YOU HAND ME....

GMC. *(To audience.)* I sold gags and sketches wherever I could—even to some burlesque comics.

(A FEMALE and a MALE BURLESQUE COMIC come on stage, from upstage right, crossing to downstage left. The male is hunched over with a kettle strapped to his back. He is carrying a chicken in one hand, using a cane and walking a dog.)

FEMALE BURLESQUE COMIC. *(To the MALE BURLESQUE COMIC.)* I just hope a big brute man like yourself doesn't get any ideas of taking liberties with a helpless maiden like myself.
MALE BURLESQUE COMIC. *(To the FEMALE BURLESQUE COMIC.)* How could I possibly take liberties with you? I've got a big kettle strapped to my back, I'm carrying a live chicken, I'm using a cane, and I'm walking my dog.
FEMALE BURLESQUE COMIC. *(To the MALE BURLESQUE COMIC.)* Well, I just hope you don't try sticking that cane in the ground, tying the dog to the cane, setting the chicken down and trapping him under that big old kettle ... because then I don't know what I'd do!

(The BURLESQUE COMICS exit downstage left.)

GMC. *(To audience.)* By age fifteen, I was not only writing our family's act—songs and sketches—I was managing it, too. And a good thing! Personally negotiating with seasoned vaudeville bookers, I was able to get as much money for all Four Cohans as they would have been willing to pay for my sister Josie alone.

(Song excerpt: The Four Cohans sing the first couple lines of the chorus of "I WANT YOU ...")

GMC, JOSIE, JERRY and NELLIE. *(Sing:)*
I WANT YOU,
YES I DO.
YOU, JUST YOU, YOU.

CAN'T YOU UNDERSTAND ME?
I DON'T CARE ABOUT
THE PRESENTS THAT YOU HAND ME....

(JERRY, NELLIE and JOSIE exit.)

GMC. *(To audience.)* And each year I was finding more promising young vaudevillians, outside the act, to showcase my material. *(ETHEL LEVEY enters from the wings, stage right.)* My songs were fresh and I got 'em to wonderful singers. Like Ethel Levey. I helped make her a star.

(GMC exits upstage left.
Song: "THE WARMEST BABY IN THE BUNCH.")

ETHEL LEVY. *(Sings with gusto:)*
WHEN THEY SEE HER COMING,
ALL THEM WENCHES TAKE A CHILL ...
DIAMONDS GLIST'NIN' ALL AROUND
AND STYLE ENOUGH TO KILL....
HER STEADY FELLAR BROKE A CRAP GAME,
DOWN IN LOUISVILLE ...
AND BUYS HER CHICKEN
EVERY DAY FOR LUNCH.

(The next two words are exclaimed, as she pantomimes throwing dice.) "Come seven!"

DREAMY EYES THAT SPARKLE
AND SHE ROLLS THEM MIGHTY CUTE....
COLORED GENT'MEN SAY THAT LADY
CERT'NY IS A "BEAUT."
"GO BROKE" THAT SHE'S A HOT POTATER.
SHE'S A RED HOT RADIATOR.
SHE'S THE WARMEST BABY IN THE BUNCH.

(The pianist begins playing another chorus starting from the top—
during this instrumental interlude, ETHEL can saucily throw in a
couple of high kicks; then ETHEL resumes singing again, starting
with the "Come seven!" line, and continues singing through the
end of the chorus, repeating the final line to wrap up the number.)

ETHEL LEVY. *(The next two words are exclaimed.)* "Come seven!" *(Sings:)*
DREAMY EYES THAT SPARKLE
AND SHE ROLLS THEM MIGHTY CUTE....
COLORED GENT'MEN SAY THAT LADY
CERT'NY IS A "BEAUT."
"GO BROKE" THAT SHE'S A HOT POTATER.
SHE'S A RED HOT RADIATOR.
SHE'S THE WARMEST BABY IN THE BUNCH....
SHE'S THE WARMEST BABY IN THE BUNCH.

(GMC enters upstage right slot. He has sheet music in his hand.)

GMC. *(To audience.)* I courted Ethel. I married Ethel.

(JOSIE enters upstage left slot.)

JOSIE. You barely knew her!
GMC. *(To audience.)* I brought her into the act.

(GMC crosses down to ETHEL.
Song: "I WANT YOU." GMC teaches the song to ETHEL. This time we hear the whole chorus. GMC sings the beginning of the chorus by himself. They finish the song together, looking at one another, thoroughly infatuated.)

GMC. *(Sings:)*
I WANT YOU,
YES I DO.
YOU, JUST YOU, YOU.

ETHEL LEVEY. *(Sings:)*
CAN'T YOU UNDERSTAND ME?
I DON'T CARE ABOUT
THE PRESENTS THAT YOU HAND ME.
I'M SO BLUE,
LONELY TOO.

GMC and ETHEL. *(Sing to one another.)*
I DON'T WANT YOUR MONEY, HONEY,
I WANT YOU.

GMC. *(To ETHEL.)* Ethel, I love writing for you. I'll give you the best songs I've got in me. I wish I could promise you more. I'm not rich, you know. Not yet. But if I could, believe me, I'd buy you a mansion. Oh, I'd buy you everything. Maybe someday....

(Song: GMC sings part of the refrain of "UNTIL MY LUCK COMES ROLLING ALONG.")

GMC. *(Sings to ETHEL:)*
WELL, ALL I CAN PROMISE IS A HAPPY DISPOSITION
AND A WILD DESIRE TO SUCCEED.
BUT I'LL ALWAYS PAY THE DAMAGE
WHEN THE RENT COMES DUE.
YOU'LL BE PROPERLY PROTECTED,
NEVER, NEVER NEGLECTED.
OH, I'D LIKE TO GIVE YOU EVERYTHING THERE IS TO GIVE,
AND WILL AS SOON AS I'M STRONG.
BUT ALL I CAN PROMISE IS A COZY LITTLE HOME.
UNTIL MY LUCK COMES ROLLING ALONG.

(The piano plays the music corresponding to the lines "Oh, I'd like to give you everything there is to give, And will as soon as I'm strong" while GMC moves about a bit. He resumes singing with the concluding lines of the refrain:)

BUT ALL I CAN PROMISE IS A COZY LITTLE HOME.
UNTIL MY LUCK COMES ROLLING ALONG.

(GMC kisses ETHEL's hand.
ETHEL and JOSIE exit. ETHEL exits downstage left; JOSIE exits upstage left.)

GMC. *(To audience.)* Josie and Ethel never got along, though. Each was jealous of the attention I paid the other. And wondered if there was room in the act for both. Women!... But I had my own work to worry about. *(Moves to center stage.)*

In those days, dancers often used to perform in place. Whether your specialty was an Irish jig or the latest American buck-and-wing hoofing, you usually stayed in the same spot, center stage, as you performed. That was the way my father, for example, performed the clog dancing he liked.

In our act, I used to do an old-time "essence of Virginia" dance, center stage, to the tune of "Coming Through the Rye." *(We hear a snatch of that familiar old melody. GMC demonstrates a bit, as he talks about dancing.)* One night, out in the sticks, I gave the conductor some new music I was working on, figuring I'd try fitting the dance to something livelier. But the conductor couldn't get the feel for what I'd written. He played it slowly, raggedly. *(The dance music we hear now, softly as GMC continues speaking, is a taste of Cohan's "The American Rag Time"—a number we will hear fully in the opening scene of Act Two—but in this scene it is played tentatively, haltingly as if the musician is really struggling to feel his way.)*

I tried stretching out my steps, to make them fit what the band was playing. I had to move about more, straining to see if I could make something fit—an exaggerated buck dance step, or a strut, tossing in an unexpected eccentric kick or two.... I scissored in there with my arms and legs, and threw back my head. The audience liked what I was trying. The next night, I experimented a little more, moved a little farther off my mark. *(GMC's dancing in this sequence— although quite tentative and embryonic—should foreshadow the kind of dancing we will see him do in the future, such as the last two numbers of Act One ["I'm a Yankee Doodle Dandy" and "Give My Regards to Broadway"] and the first number of Act Two ["The American Ragtime"]. We are witnessing here the early development of a style, making greater use of the stage, that we will see in fuller, far more self-assured form in GMC's subsequent appearances in the show. In this sequence, the performer can haltingly strut a bit, perhaps offer a little eccentric kick or two, moving a little outside of the center-stage area. The performer should only give us a brief, exploratory hint of what we will see, more fully realized, later in the show. He can't give everything away to the audience at this point; he must simply suggest an artist beginning to find a style all his own. His spoken words can be modified a bit, if need be, to jibe with the moves he is making.*

Cohan became a dynamic song-and-dance man with various idiosyncratic steps in his repertoire. In his years as a Broadway star, he could move about the stage engagingly with what reviewers referred to as his "loping, kangaroo walk" or his "bent-knee-action walk." Or he could stride commandingly, leaning forward, up on his toes. He could unexpectedly burst into what appreciative critics termed a "ridiculous little skip." He could run from one side of the stage to the other, mounting the proscenium arch, turning off of it—

and sometimes run across the stage again to ascend the proscenium arch on the other side of the stage as well, turn off of it and run back to center stage. Such Cohan moves may be evoked later in the show. Right now, we're just catching glimpses of an artist in the process of finding himself. But the tentative moves we see him experimenting with in this scene must relate to the far more polished moves we'll see him make later in the show. GMC continues to audience.)

Out there in the boonies, in the months that followed—experimenting with new melodies, new moves, different ways to walk—I was working out a style of my own.... *(Finishes his dance-move experimenting. The music trails off. He moves to center stage.)*

You know, my family's act was second to none. Over twenty years, the Cohans had built a following in every part the U.S. It was strong, and it was growing. I finally hammered out a contract with B. F. Keith, the biggest, toughest vaudeville booker, guaranteeing us top billing wherever we played. *(B. F. KEITH enters from downstage left.)* Then we headed to Boston—where I found us billed dead last. I read him the riot act.

KEITH. *(To GMC.)* It's some mistake, some press agent's or sign painter's mistake, not mine.

GMC. It isn't mine, either. You expect me not to care if you break a contract. I remember a time, years ago, when you had to borrow money from my father to meet your payroll. He gave you $600, without questioning it.

KEITH. *(To GMC.)* Your *father* never gave anyone in this business trouble, Cohan.

GMC. That's why I'm running the act now. For all those years, he let the likes of you take advantage. Those days are over.

KEITH. I understand now, it's a shakedown.

GMC. *(Crossing to KEITH.)* Just because of that crack, I'll make you a promise right now—no member of the Cohan family will ever play for you again. *(To audience.)* And we never did. At age twenty-one, I walked out on the man who in those days provided our family with half of our employment all year. I fought with managers and agents from coast to coast. B. F. Keith wasn't the only one.

KEITH. You have convinced me of the necessity of capital punishment.

(KEITH exits, downstage left.)

GMC. *(To audience.)* When the only offers of work we were getting were for my sister alone, or for my parents as a duo—no one wanted Georgie; Georgie was "trouble"—I took it as a sign the time had come to conquer Broadway. I headed to New York, to create a show that I could star in, and the whole family, and my wife Ethel, could be in.

In those days, the most respected shows on Broadway were imports from England and the Continent. People loved operettas set in mythical European kingdoms, which bored me silly. I convinced A. L. Erlanger, one of the biggest producers on Broadway, to back me on my first full-length show. *(ERLANGER enters from the wings stage right.)* He knew the Cohans had a following in vaudeville. But he was gambling. To the leading New York theater critics, vaudeville was considered lower class. And there was certainly nothing European about what I was writing. It was as American in spirit as our young president, Teddy Roosevelt.

ERLANGER. *(To GMC.)* What's the name of your show?

GMC. *(To ERLANGER.)* "Little Johnny Jones." Wait till you see it. It's the best thing I've ever done. *(To audience.)* To tell the truth, I hadn't done it at all. I was far too busy to get down to the actual writing until about ten days before the rehearsal call. All I'd thought of so far was the title, but that struck me as being a hundred per cent "box office."

ERLANGER. *(To audience.)* George wrote the first act in one day, brought it to me on a shirt cuff the next morning, and read it standing up. I asked him to bring round the other two cuffs as soon as he got them out of the laundry.

(ERLANGER exits into the wings stage right.)

GMC. *(To audience.)* At the building where I'd rented an office, I met a producer just starting out—Sam Harris. *(HARRIS enters upstage left.)* I asked him if he'd like to buy into a surefire hit.

SAM HARRIS. *(To audience.)* It didn't take long for me to believe in him. He was the most confident man I'd ever met. Even the way he walked impressed me—leaning forward as if he couldn't wait to get where he was going. I thought, "This is the future of the American theater." We shook hands and formed Cohan and Harris Productions.

(SAM HARRIS crosses to shake GMC's hand.)

GMC. *(To audience.)* I never believed in written contracts. If a man's word is good, a handshake is enough. That's the kind of a little guy I am. *(A phone rings offstage from upstage left.)* Sam Harris was one of the only people I ever fully trusted, outside of my family.

(A YOUNG ACTOR comes out from upstage left.)

YOUNG ACTOR: There's a call for you, Mr. Cohan.
GMC. *(To audience.)* Sam got a kick out of the way I'd occasionally have characters speak directly to the audience. And every now and then remind the audience that we're in the world of the theater—*my* world, if you will—not real life.
YOUNG ACTOR. It's important you take that call, Mr. Cohan.
GMC. I'll take it. *(To audience.)* Although if the phone rang for a character in one of my plays, I might have the character look straight at the audience and acknowledge: The playwright is probably making that phone ring about now, just to get me offstage for a costume change.

(GMC exits upstage left, arm around shoulder of YOUNG ACTOR, so he can change into jockey outfit.)

SAM HARRIS. *(To audience, crossing to center.)* George would break the fourth wall with abandon. I read his script pages before anyone else. I liked the way he'd throw in moments like this:

(Two ACTORS enter from upstage left slot; they have the following brief exchange while moving downstage, to exit downstage right.)

ACTOR #1. *(Addressing the other actor while pointing ahead.)* Officer, arrest that man!
JERRY COHAN. *(Playing a police officer, addressing ACTOR #1.)* We can't do that. We're barely halfway through Act Two. The villain doesn't get caught until around 11:00. It's been going on like that for years and years.

(ACTOR #1 shrugs as if to say, "Now I get it," and exits.)

SAM HARRIS. *(To audience.)* He'd bring me pages of dialogue, scrawled in pencil. And I'd read ...

(JOSIE COHAN and YOUNG ACTOR enter from upstage right slot; they have the following brief exchange while moving downstage to exit downstage left.)

JOSIE. *(Playing a gal in a scene.)* I'm sorry Steve, but it's all cold. Goodbye!
YOUNG ACTOR. Goodbye!
JOSIE. Don't you dare come to the door of my room.
YOUNG ACTOR. I don't even know the number of your room.
JOSIE. Don't you dare come to room 502. It's all over, Steve. You go my way and I'll go mine.

(She exits sobbing downstage left.)

YOUNG ACTOR. *(To audience.)* I'm glad *that's* over.

(He exits downstage left.)

SAM HARRIS. *(To audience.)* Unlike most musicals of the day, "Little Johnny Jones" had a significant plot. He wrote about an American jockey in London, proudly entering the English Derby. *(MEMBERS OF THE ENSEMBLE begin filing onstage, getting in position of the "Little Johnny Jones" numbers.)* George and I put everything we had, or could borrow, into "Little Johnny Jones." By the time of the show's first performance, we were down to our last $50.

But all that irresistible confidence I saw in George offstage, he projected the moment he stepped onto the stage.

(GMC enters from upstage right in jockey outfit, coming to downstage center while admiring gals gaze at him.)

ETHEL LEVEY. *(Who's playing a girl in the cast of "Little Johnny Jones" and is looking at GMC adoringly.)* What makes you Americans so proud of your country?
GMC. *Other* countries....
AGNES NOLAN. *(Who's playing another girl in the cast, also looking at GMC adoringly.)* Do you really think you have a chance, Johnny, competing against British jockeys on British soil?
GMC. Girls! Girls! You really want a tip on the race? Pawn your jewelry, go in hock! Play Yankee Doodle to win. I'm gonna give America the English Derby cup.

GEORGE M. COHAN: IN HIS OWN WORDS

(Song: "THE YANKEE DOODLE BOY"—also known as "I'm a Yankee Doodle Dandy." This is a major number of the show. GMC sings and dances with great charm and pride. He primarily plays it to the audience. He is telling all of us—not just the other characters on the stage—who he is. In the course of this number he strides the stage with that leaning-forward, up-on-his-toes Cohan walk and does a turn off the proscenium arch or wall at stage left. [As a performer, Cohan was known for making use of the proscenium arch; he could sort of run up it a bit, do a turn off of it. The performer should evoke Cohan's tradition of making use of the proscenium arch. As a singer/dancer, the whole stage was Cohan's to use, and it is essential that reality be represented.] GMC will sing the first verse and refrain and then the second verse and refrain all by himself [with the chorus coming in to sing a few brief phrases, as marked]. The other MEMBERS OF THE ENSEMBLE stand and watch GMC as he sings. On the next performance of the refrain, the entire ENSEMBLE sings along with GMC; some movement can be added. The concluding performance of the refrain is largely danced, with everyone coming in the sing the last few lines together.)

GMC. *(Sings brightly:)*
I'M THE KID THAT'S ALL THE CANDY.
I'M A YANKEE DOODLE DANDY.
I'M GLAD I AM.

CHORUS. *(Sings:)*
SO'S UNCLE SAM.

GMC. *(Sings:)*
I'M A REAL LIVE YANKEE DOODLE,
MADE MY NAME AND FAME AND BOODLE,
JUST LIKE MISTER DOODLE DID,
BY RIDING ON A PONY.
I LOVE TO LISTEN TO THE DIXIE STRAIN.
"I LONG TO SEE THE GIRL I LEFT BEHIND ME."
AND THAT AIN'T NO JOSH.
SHE'S A YANKEE, BY GOSH.

CHORUS. *(Sings:)*
OH, SAY CAN YOU SEE?

GMC. *(Sings:)*
ANYTHING ABOUT A YANKEE THAT'S A PHONY?

I'M A YANKEE DOODLE DANDY.
A YANKEE DOODLE, DO OR DIE;
A REAL LIVE NEPHEW OF MY UNCLE SAM'S,
BORN ON THE FOURTH OF JULY.
I'VE GOT A YANKEE DOODLE SWEETHEART,
SHE'S MY YANKEE DOODLE JOY.
YANKEE DOODLE CAME TO LONDON, JUST TO RIDE THE
 PONIES.
I AM THE YANKEE DOODLE BOY.

FATHER'S NAME WAS HEZIKIAH,
MOTHER'S NAME WAS ANN MARIA.
YANKS THROUGH AND THROUGH.

CHORUS. *(Sings:)*
RED, WHITE AND BLUE.

GMC. *(Sings:)*
FATHER WAS SO YANKEE-HEARTED,
WHEN THE SPANISH WAR WAS STARTED,
HE SLIPPED ON HIS UNIFORM AND HOPPED UPON A PONY.
MY MOTHER'S MOTHER WAS A YANKEE TRUE,
MY FATHER'S FATHER WAS A YANKEE TOO.
AND THAT'S GOING SOME,
FOR THE YANKEES, BY GUM.

CHORUS. *(Sings:)*
OH, SAY CAN YOU SEE
 GMC. *(Sings:)*
ANYTHING ABOUT MY PEDIGREE THAT'S PHONY?

GMC and CHORUS. *(Sing—with GMC singing the words. as given below, in the first-person, and the chorus singing them in the third person; that is to say, if he sings "I'm a Yankee Doodle Dandy," "I've Got a Yankee Doodle Sweetheart," the chorus backing him will be singing, "He's a Yankee Doodle Dandy," "He's Got a Yankee Doodle Sweetheart," etc.)*
I'M A YANKEE DOODLE DANDY.

A YANKEE DOODLE,
DO OR DIE.
A REAL LIVE NEPHEW
OF MY UNCLE SAM'S.
BORN ON THE FOURTH OF JULY.
I'VE GOT A YANKEE DOODLE SWEETHEART,
SHE'S MY YANKEE DOODLE JOY.
YANKEE DOODLE CAME TO LONDON
JUST TO RIDE THE PONIES.
I AM THE YANKEE DOODLE BOY.

(Dance break. The pianist begins playing the melody of the refrain again, all the way through. And this time GMC and company dance. They resume singing with the line, "I've got a Yankee Doodle Sweetheart," and sing the rest of the refrain to the conclusion. Once again, GMC sings in the first-person: "I've got a Yankee Doodle Sweetheart, she's my Yankee Doodle joy ... I am the Yankee Doodle Boy;" the chorus sings the same lines but in the third-person: "He's got a Yankee Doodle Sweetheart, she's his Yankee Doodle joy ... He is the Yankee Doodle Boy," etc.)

GMC and CHORUS. *(Sing:)*
I'VE GOT A YANKEE DOODLE SWEETHEART,
SHE'S MY YANKEE DOODLE JOY.
YANKEE DOODLE CAME TO LONDON
JUST TO RIDE THE PONIES.
I AM THE YANKEE DOODLE BOY.

SAM HARRIS. *(To audience.)* That night, I was witnessing the birth of modern American musical comedy. Audiences had never seen anything like this. At a time when America was finding its way in the world, first asserting itself as a world power, here was young George M. capturing that mood. All the bravado.... With an occasional moment of self-doubt thrown in. *(As SAM talks, GMC, downstage center with back to audience, is facing throng of admiring gals. To audience.)* In the musical, Johnny Jones loses the English Derby. The race has been fixed. And he's been framed. Johnny is disgraced. The adoring crowds desert him.

(As HARRIS speaks we see the others begin to desert Johnny Jones [GMC].)

BRITISH RACING OFFICIAL. We accuse you of throwing the race. We're barring you from ever riding again.

(Song: GMC reprises "THE YANKEE DOODLE BOY" [also known as "I'm a Yankee Doodle Dandy"] starting from the words, "I've got a Yankee Doodle sweetheart"—this time talk/singing it slowly, mournfully, a shaken man.)

GMC. *(Sings:)*
I'VE GOT A YANKEE DOODLE SWEETHEART,
SHE'S MY YANKEE DOODLE JOY.
YANKEE DOODLE CAME TO LONDON, JUST TO RIDE THE PONIES.
I AM THAT YANKEE DOODLE BOY.

SAM HARRIS. *(To audience.)* His friends will sail back to America without him.
OFFSTAGE MALE VOICE. *(Done by JERRY COHAN.)* All aboard!

(The fickle friends go by, cold-shouldering him as they exit, except for the one played by ETHEL LEVEY.)

ETHEL LEVEY. Good luck, Johnny. I still believe in you.
GMC. Thanks, kid. That means a lot. *(Calls after her.)* I'm not leaving England till I've cleared my name.

(JERRY and NELLIE COHAN enter from upstage right.)

MAN. *(Played by JERRY COHAN.)* You wait here at Southampton Pier, Johnny. We hope to find in Anstey's cabin certain papers that will prove you innocent of throwing the race. If we find them, we'll set off a skyrocket from the ship. You wait here. Watch for the skyrocket, Johnny.

(JERRY and NELLIE exit downstage right, leaving GMC alone on stage. Song: "GIVE MY REGARDS TO BROADWAY.")

GMC. *(Sings slowly, wistfully:)*
GIVE MY REGARDS TO BROADWAY,
REMEMBER ME TO HERALD SQUARE.

TELL ALL THE GANG AT FORTY-SECOND STREET
THAT I WILL SOON BE THERE.
WHISPER OF HOW I'M YEARNING
TO MINGLE WITH THE OLD-TIME THRONG.
GIVE MY REGARDS TO OLD BROADWAY
AND SAY THAT I'LL BE THERE E'ER LONG.

(The lights dim, signifying time's passage. We hear a skyrocket ascending and exploding; GMC is watching the skyrocket—looking out and above the audience. The skyrocket may be suggested by the use of sound effects—and/or ascending notes played on the piano—plus strobe lighting when it goes off. GMC's mood changes the moment we hear the skyrocket go off.
Song: "GIVE MY REGARDS TO BROADWAY." Highly upbeat. GMC sings, and then dances, this number triumphantly. He commands the whole stage, his dancing bringing him into contact briefly with the proscenium arch or wall at stage left. This number is another major moment of the show, and should bring the First Act to a strong conclusion.)

GMC. *(Sings exuberantly:)*
GIVE MY REGARDS TO BROADWAY,
REMEMBER ME TO HERALD SQUARE.
TELL ALL THE GANG AT FORTY-SECOND STREET
THAT I WILL SOON BE THERE.
WHISPER OF HOW I'M YEARNING
TO MINGLE WITH THE OLD-TIME THRONG.
GIVE MY REGARDS TO OLD BROADWAY
AND SAY THAT I'LL BE THERE E'ER LONG.

(Dance break. The pianist plays the entire refrain through one more time as GMC tap dances to it. He resumes singing for the last two lines, stretching out the last five words for a big finish.)

GMC. *(Sings)*
GIVE MY REGARDS TO OLD BROADWAY
AND SAY THAT I'LL BE THERE E'ER LONG.

(Blackout.)

END OF ACT I

AN ALTERNATE WAY OF ENDING THE SCENE

If desired, and it is practical—if this is being performed in a theater with a traveler curtain—GMC can conclude this scene by pulling the curtain closed himself. In this case, he prances or struts to the music, tugging the curtain closed, moving from stage left to center, finally disappearing behind the closed curtain. This business of waggishly pulling the front curtain closed was in Cohan's repertoire.

ACT II

(Song: "THE AMERICAN RAG TIME." After seven introductory bars [quoting from the melody of "The Man Who Owns Broadway"], the chorus of "The American Rag Time" is heard three times. The first chorus is strictly instrumental. We hear the high-spirited music played with polish and verve; members of the ensemble—minus GMC—come onstage and dance to the music. Then, on the second chorus, the members of the ensemble—minus GMC—sing as well as dance to the music. So we first hear just the melody—which GMC had been toying with in Act One, when he was developing new dance moves—and then get to hear the catchy, patriotic words that he's written. Among those singing and dancing in the second chorus are JOSIE COHAN, ETHEL LEVEY and AGNES NOLAN. Finally, GMC—dressed in a dapper suit—is brought on stage and into the production number on the third chorus, to sing and dance with the ensemble, and close the number with élan.

The first two choruses provide a buildup for his entrance. The audience should feel that the embryonic ideas for music and dance GMC had been working on in Act One have really developed into something; Cohan has "arrived." One signature Cohan bit of business, which should be incorporated into this sequence if possible, was Cohan's jauntily marching across the stage, leaning forward, carrying an American flag over one shoulder the way a soldier might carry a rifle. While doing so, he could offer the audience a friendly wink—another Cohanesque touch.)

THE ENSEMBLE. *(Sings spiritedly:)*
IT'S THE AMERICAN RAG TIME,
WITH A RAGGY, RAGGY RING.
IT'S THE AMERICAN RAG TIME,
WITH A PATRIOTIC SWING.
I'VE HEARD THE MERRY WIDOW
AND THE CANDY KID-DO,
BUT GIVE ME THE ZAM, ZAM, ZAM!

THAT PLEASES UNCLE SAM,
I'M CRAZY, YES I AM,
FOR AMERICAN RAG TIME,
IS THE ONLY TUNE WILL DO;
THE AMERICAN RAG TIME,
WELL, IT THRILLS YOU THROUGH AND THROUGH....
SO, TAKE ALL YOUR GRAND OPERA SCORES,
AND BACK TO THE TALL WITH THEM, ALL FOR YOURS,
I WANT THE AMERICAN RAG TIME.

GMC and ENSEMBLE. *(Sing:)*
IT'S THE AMERICAN RAG TIME,
WITH A RAGGY, RAGGY RING.
IT'S THE AMERICAN RAG TIME,
WITH A PATRIOTIC SWING.
I'VE HEARD THE MERRY WIDOW
AND THE CANDY KID-DO,
BUT GIVE ME THE ZAM, ZAM, ZAM!
THAT PLEASES UNCLE SAM,
I'M CRAZY, YES I AM,
FOR AMERICAN RAG TIME,
IS THE ONLY TUNE WILL DO;
THE AMERICAN RAG TIME,
WELL, IT THRILLS YOU THROUGH AND THROUGH....
SO, TAKE ALL YOUR GRAND OPERA SCORES,
AND BACK TO THE TALL WITH THEM, ALL FOR YOURS,
I WANT THE AMERICAN RAG TIME.

(MEMBERS OF THE ENSEMBLE exit.)

GMC. *(Curtain speech to audience:)* My father thanks you, my mother thanks you, my sister thanks you, and I thank you.

(SAM HARRIS enters upstage left.)

SAM HARRIS. *(To audience.)* The public took Cohan to its heart. A whole rising generation of Americans idolized him. *(SAM HARRIS crosses down left.)* But when George first hit Broadway, the critical establishment—the old-guard critics—turned their noses up at him. They wanted theater that was refined, genteel, that followed European models. George was young. He was bold. He was

American.

(SAM HARRIS exits downstage left. GMC moves to downstage center.)

GMC. *(To audience.)* I remember well every review. One critic of "Little Johnny Jones"—who hadn't been too crazy about my work in vaudeville, either—sniffed:

(JERRY COHAN enters from upstage right. He takes a position upstage right.)

JERRY. *(To audience.)* "He has written a dozen and a half musical numbers whose distinguishing feature is ginger. In fact, there is more ginger than music. It is all very Cohanesque."

GMC. *(To audience.)* One of New York's foremost dramatic experts termed me:

(NELLIE COHAN enters from the slot upstage right and takes a position upstage center, in line with JERRY.)

NELLIE. *(To audience.)* "A swaggering, impudent, noisy vaudevillian, entirely out of place in first-class theaters."

GMC. *(To audience.)* James Metcalfe, the veteran drama critic of *Life Magazine*, complained:

(CRITIC enters from upstage left, and takes a position upstage left, in line with JERRY and NELLIE.)

CRITIC. *(To audience.)* "In the character which he has created for himself, he presumably typifies the ideal of American young manhood. He makes him a vulgar, cheap, blatant, ill-mannered, flashily dressed, insolent smart-aleck, who for some reason unexplainable on any basis of common sense, good taste, or even ordinary decency, appeals to the imagination and apparent approval of large American audiences. As a living character in any American town, it is hardly to be conceived that he would not be driven out as a public nuisance and a pernicious example to the youth of this country."

GMC. *(To audience.)* One fellow in Cincinnati proclaimed:

JERRY. *(To audience.)* "Cohan is a disease ... and the Yankee

Doodle fever is spreading far and wide."

GMC. *(To audience.)* The review that hurt me the most came from a critic in Providence, my own home town.

CRITIC. *(To audience.)* "Young Mr. Cohan has done things to the 'drama' that would cause even the audacious George Bernard Shaw to gasp. 'Musical comedies' are common, but this is the first known attempt to construct a 'musical melodrama.' There is more than a barrelful of plot, and it keeps cropping out in chunks in the middle of alleged music and eccentric dancing in a way to make a sane person hold his throbbing head. Any attempt to describe it would be futile; life is too short."

GMC. *(To audience.)* "I'll get even with Providence for this," I vowed. It was ten solid years before I played the town again.

(SAM HARRIS enters from the wings stage right.)

SAM HARRIS. *(To audience.)* Don't let George fool you, though. There were also astute younger observers who definitely recognized his importance. As Oscar Hammerstein acknowledged:

(JERRY steps a bit downstage to deliver his lines.)

JERRY. *(To audience.)* "The whole nation was confident of its superiority, its moral virtue, its happy isolation.... Cohan's genius was to say simply what everybody was subconsciously feeling."

SAM HARRIS. *(To audience.)* One admiring reviewer, Gilbert Ellery, wrote of George:

(The CRITIC steps a bit downstage to deliver his lines.)

CRITIC. *(To audience.)* "He represents the spirit and energy of the 20th century—a concentrated essence, four-cylinder power."

SAM HARRIS. *(To audience.)* Another critic, C. R. Trousdale, observed:

(NELLIE steps a bit downstage to deliver her lines.)

NELLIE. *(To audience.)* "Cohan has introduced a whole new conception of delivery, tempo, subject matter ..."

GMC. *(To audience.)* Amy Leslie of the *Chicago Daily News* liked my "big, soulful eyes that speak music ... and glow with fun."

Awwwww....

SAM HARRIS. *(To audience.)* The *New York Sun* called the directness with which Cohan hurled ideas at the audience "revolutionary." George Jean Nathan, at the start of an extraordinarily distinguished career as a critic, championed Cohan. He compared his sense of construction to Euripedes.' And he noted it was Cohan "who first brought the quick-step species of direction into our theater—and brought it to perfection."

Another reviewer, Cody L. Green, put it this way:

NELLIE. *(To audience.)* "It is quite obvious that Mr. Cohan's strict directions for a musical comedy success are: 'Keep moving. It doesn't make much difference what you do, so long as you keep moving.'"

(Everyone except GMC exits, downstage or into the wings. GMC moves to a spot, downstage left, and observes.)

Song:. MEMBERS OF THE ENSEMBLE—including JOSIE COHAN, ETHEL LEVEY and AGNES NOLAN—dance across the stage from upstage left to downstage right, singing one brisk chorus or less—this number can be trimmed as the director sees fit; 16 bars may well be sufficient—of "DANCING MY WORRIES AWAY" as if to illustrate the "keep-moving" idea.

MEMBERS OF THE ENSEMBLE. *(Sing briskly:)*
WE KEEP ON DANCING,
WE LOVE TO BE DANCING,
WE LOVE TO BE DANCING
NIGHT AND DAY.
DANCING, TO ME IS ENTRANCING.
I'M HAPPY WHEN THE MUSIC'S JAZZING AWAY.
WE KEEP ON DANCING,
WE'RE PRANCING AND DANCING
AS LONG AS A BAND WILL EVER PLAY.
WINE AND SONG
WE LEAVE BEHIND US.
ALL NIGHT LONG,
YOU'RE SURE TO FIND US,
DANCING, WE LOVE TO BE DANCING,
WE LOVE TO BE DANCING OUR WORRIES AWAY!

(The MEMBERS OF THE ENSEMBLE exit.)

GMC. *(To audience.)* The first rule of musical comedy: When in doubt, dance!

I brought "Little Johnny Jones" back from the road to Broadway—the only such Broadway comeback I ever witnessed. The show's hits were being whistled, brass-banded, hand-organed, and phonographed throughout the U.S.

While starring in "Little Johnny Jones," I wrote and directed "Forty Five Minutes from Broadway," featuring Fay Templeton—the biggest female star on Broadway—and young Victor Moore. I set the musical in New Rochelle, New York. Oh, I gave New Rochelle an awful ribbing for being provincial. The town fathers thanked me for making it famous.

(GMC exits downstage left. While offstage GMC can change out of his tap shoes into regular character shoes. The MALE SINGER and FAY TEMPLETON enter from upstage slot, left.
Song: The MALE SINGER [VICTOR MOORE], FAY TEMPLETON and CHORUS perform the "FORTY-FIVE MINUTES FROM BROADWAY.")

MALE SINGER and FAY TEMPLETON *(Sing together with a lilt:)*
ONLY FORTY-FIVE MINUTES FROM BROADWAY,
THINK OF THE CHANGES IT BRINGS.
FOR THE SHORT TIME IT TAKES, WHAT A DIFF'RENCE IT MAKES
IN THE WAYS OF THE PEOPLE AND THINGS.
OH! WHAT A FINE BUNCH OF REUBENS,
OH! WHAT A JAY ATMOSPHERE.
THEY HAVE WHISKERS LIKE HAY, AND IMAGINE BROADWAY
ONLY FORTY-FIVE MINUTES FROM HERE.

FAY TEMPLETON. *(Sings:)*
ONLY FORTY-FIVE MINUTES FROM BROADWAY,
NOT A CAFE IN THE TOWN.
MALE SINGER. *(Sings:)*
OH, THE PLACE IS A BIRD, NO ONE HERE EVER HEARD
OF DELMONICO, RECTOR, OR BROWNE!
FAY TEMPLETON. *(Sings:)*
WITH A TEN-DOLLAR BILL YOU'RE A SPENDTHRIFT,

MALE SINGER. *(Sings:)*
IF YOU OPEN A BOTTLE OF BEER,
YOU'RE A SPORT, SO THEY SAY, AND IMAGINE BROADWAY
ONLY FORTY-FIVE MINUTES FROM HERE.

(The pianist begins playing the refrain again, and a half-dozen gals enter from upstage left to dance. The MALE SINGER and FAY TEMPLETON resume singing on the line, "Oh! What a fine bunch of reubens …" and finish the song.)

MALE SINGER and FAY TEMPLETON *(Sing:)*
OH! WHAT A FINE BUNCH OF REUBENS,
OH! WHAT A JAY ATMOSPHERE.
THEY HAVE WHISKERS LIKE HAY, AND IMAGINE
    BROADWAY
ONLY FORTY-FIVE MINUTES FROM HERE.

(The MALE SINGER exits.
Song: "MARY'S A GRAND OLD NAME")

FAY TEMPLETON. *(Sings:)*
MY MOTHER'S NAME WAS MARY,
SHE WAS SO GOOD AND TRUE;
BECAUSE HER NAME WAS MARY,
SHE CALLED ME MARY TOO.
SHE WASN'T GAY OR AIRY,
BUT PLAIN AS SHE COULD BE.
I HATE TO MEET A MARY
WHO CALLS HERSELF MARIE.

FOR IT IS MARY, MARY,
PLAIN AS ANY NAME CAN BE;
BUT WITH PROPRIETY, SOCIETY
WILL SAY MARIE.
BUT IT WAS MARY, MARY,
LONG BEFORE THE FASHIONS CAME;
AND THERE IS SOMETHING THERE
THAT SOUNDS SO SQUARE,
IT'S A GRAND OLD NAME.

(The pianist begins playing part of the refrain again, starting with the

line corresponding to "But it was Mary ...." FAY TEMPLETON resumes singing on the line "And there is something there ...")

FAY TEMPLETON. *(Sings:)*
AND THERE IS SOMETHING THERE
THAT SOUNDS SO SQUARE,
T'S A GRAND OLD NAME.

(FAY TEMPLETON exits upstage left slot. GMC enters from downstage left.)

GMC. *(To audience.)* Critics were divided over "Forty-Five Minutes from Broadway." The fellow in Columbus called it "a feeble attempt at musical comedy," while the *Chicago Tribune* proclaimed it "one of the best song plays in twenty years." I ran these two notices side by side in the Chicago papers as an ad.... The Columbus critic, poor baby, lost his job.

(SAM HARRIS enters from upstage right, crosses downstage taking a position near GMC.)

SAM HARRIS. *(To audience.)* As George took his shows throughout the country, even newspapers with mixed feelings acknowledged he was a phenomenon. The *Ohio State Journal* ran its review of his new show *on the front page*. And American youth took to imitating him: his jaunty stride, his way of talking, confidentially, out of one side of his mouth. Dancers across America took to wearing their hair long, Cohan-style.

(ERLANGER enters from wings stage right.)

ERLANGER. *(To audience.)* How could anyone not love George? He would always kid me, but I never minded. He had such natural charm. You just wanted to say, "Come into my garden; I'd like my roses to meet you." And George thought *big*. Which is another reason we got along. I always thought big myself. You know, when another playwright brought me a show called "Little Miss Springtime," I changed the title to "Miss Springtime." I told him nothing "little" could ever appear at *Erlanger's* theater!

SAM HARRIS. *(To audience.)* George's exuberant musicals—more unified in spirit than any Broadway had seen before—were simply projections of his own personality.

ERLANGER. *(To audience.)* George was always going, going, going! I'd tell him he worked too much! I'd tell him he was young; he needed to get out more, have some hijinks, find new ways to have fun. That night he woke me up; in the middle of the night he came 'round, knocking at my door.

(GMC crosses to ERLANGER.)

GMC. *(To ERLANGER.)* Abe Erlanger, I've a confession. I *do* find ways to have my fun. I'll let you in on it.... Sam and I are members of a very secret, very exclusive fraternal organization. If you want to join, there's an $80 initiation fee, for contingencies and such. You'll learn more in due time.

(Lights shift.)

ERLANGER. George, two weeks ago I gave you $80 for contingencies. And I still haven't learned a thing.
GMC. Trust me, Abe! If any contingencies should arise where Sam or I need another $80 fast, you'll be the first to know!
ERLANGER. George and Sam became so successful, so quickly, they didn't need my help in producing anymore. But I never missed the opening of a Cohan show, from "Hello, Broadway!" to "The Song and Dance Man" to "The Little Millionaire."

(ERLANGER exits.)

SAM HARRIS. *(To audience)* George did every job a person could do in the theater—he sang, he danced, he acted, he directed, he choreographed, he produced, he wrote his show's books, music, and lyrics. That drove some critics mad. They charged him with being egotistical.

(SAM HARRIS exits downstage left.)

GMC. *(To audience.)* I formed a theatrical newspaper, "The Spotlight," to rebut them. We ran weekly attacks on all unfriendly critics, which I wrote and signed myself. I responded to that critic's charge that I was an egotist:

I write my own songs because I write better songs than anyone else that I know of. I publish these songs because they bring greater royalties than any other class of music sold in this country. I write my own plays because I have not yet seen plays from the pens of other authors that seem as good as the plays I write. I produce my own plays because I'm as good a theatrical manager as any other man in that line. I dance because I know I'm the best dancer in the country. I sing because I can sing my own songs better than any other man on the stage. I play the leading parts in my plays because I think I'm the best actor available. I pay myself the biggest salary ever paid a song and dance comedian because I know I deserve it.

But believe me when I say, I am not an egotist.

A Toledo critic said:

(The CRITIC enters from downstage left, says his line and exits.)

CRITIC. *(To audience.)* "I guess that guy doesn't care what we say about him so long as we keep his name before the public."

GMC. *(To audience.)* I could hardly believe that any guy from Toldeo could be smart enough to figure it out.

(JERRY COHAN enters from upstage left slot.)

JERRY COHAN. *(To GMC.)* You've achieved more success than anyone else in the show business. What more do you want?

GMC. *(To audience.)* Everybody loved my father—his gentleness, his grace, his kindness. They used to bill him as a "songster, dancer, *philosopher*...." A wise man. I told him I *enjoyed* jousting with my critics.

JERRY COHAN. Why should you care what critics might think? So much is more important in life. The friendships you make....

GMC. I tell anyone who asks: I have just five friends in this world I could really count on—and I'm not too sure about one of them.

Anyway, I need to keep busy. I have to make sure there will always be work for the Four Cohans ... or Five Cohans, if you count Ethel.

JERRY COHAN. Son, don't worry about providing work for me anymore. It's getting harder for me just to memorize lines.

GMC. Pop! The day will never come when you'll forget the words of a Cohan song. You're going to love the songs I'm writing for our next show, "The Honeymooners."

(GMC walks JERRY offstage.
Song: MEMBERS OF THE ENSEMBLE, led by the MALE SINGER, enter from upstage left slot to sing a chorus of "SWEET POPULARITY.")

MEMBERS OF THE ENSEMBLE. *(Sing nonchalantly:)*
SWEET POPULARITY, GLORIOUS POPULARITY,
I'D RATHER HAVE THAN A MILLION
OR A BILLION
OR QUADRILLION.
WHY WEALTH TO CONTENTMENT'S A PARODY.
I ONLY USE IT FOR CHARITY.
MY PLEASURES ARE FEW,
EV'RYTHING THAT I DO
IS FOR POPULARITY.

(Brief instrumental interlude.)

MY PLEASURES ARE FEW,
EV'RYTHING THAT I DO
IS FOR POPULARITY.

(The MEMBERS OF THE ENSEMBLE exit.
SAM HARRIS enters from wings, stage right.)

SAM HARRIS. *(To audience.)* George became the leader of the theatrical community. In what free time he had, he held court at the Lambs Club and the Friars Club. His handouts helped countless show folk in times of need. He was the softest touch on Broadway.

(GMC enters from upstage left.)

GMC. Remember Davey Barth from our first musical, Sam?
SAM HARRIS. Is he still on the Cohan dole?
GMC. He came round today, saying he'd like to get married, and was wondering if I could double my weekly handout.
SAM HARRIS. Don't tell me you said yes?
GMC. Hell no! I told him I wouldn't raise what I give him by more than 50%.
SAM HARRIS. *(To audience.)* I got George a good business manager to keep him from giving away all his money. But George

often found ways to outsmart us. He'd write words and music, gratis, for performers he liked. Let charities perform his shows for free. He gave his smash hit play, "Get-Rich-Quick Wallingford" to his mother as a Christmas present. All the money it made went to Nellie, not him.

GMC. *(To SAM HARRIS.)* No regrets.

SAM HARRIS. *(To audience.)* George liked saying he was never terribly fond of actors. But he spent more time with actors than with his own wife.

GMC. *(To audience.)* Well, I was more of a man's man. I liked the clubs. Oh, I built a home out in Great Neck. But that was more the wife's territory.

SAM HARRIS. *(To audience.)* Show people were forever bringing him their problems.

(A DISTRAUGHT ACTOR enters from upstage right.)

DISTRAUGHT ACTOR. George, I just came to say goodbye. My Norma has left me for another guy. I've bought a gun, and I'm going to end it all. Don't try to talk me out of it! I've written a note that will explain everything.

(The DISTRAUGHT ACTOR hands him the note.)

GMC. *(Looking over the note.)* Well, if I can be frank, kid.... This note that you've written—honestly, it could use a little work.

DISTRAUGHT ACTOR. What are you talking about?

GMC. There's no style to this note. A lot of drama, but no style. See, you always want to aim for both.

DISTRAUGHT ACTOR. Where? Where is it wrong?

GMC. Well, here—where you're going on about how even in the winter, when you were broke, you bought your gal flowers.... We can phrase that more gracefully. How about if we say: "I gave you roses in December...." Now *that* has a lilt to it.

DISTRAUGHT ACTOR. But, but—

GMC. And you can't end your first two sentences with the same word. You can't rhyme "pal" with "pal."

DISTRAUGHT ACTOR. I wasn't trying for a *rhyme scheme*.

GMC. Listen, we really need to work on this together.

(GMC walks the distraught actor offstage; the ACTOR exits downstage left.)

SAM HARRIS. *(To audience.)* By night's end, George had turned the suicide note into a song—which became a hit. Years later that grateful actor would serve as one of George's own pallbearers.

GMC. *(To audience.)* "Roses in December" *was* a damned good title for a song.

(ISIDORE WITMARK enters from upstage right slot carrying a hefty manuscript.)

ISIDORE WITMARK. George! My dear George!

GMC. *(To SAM HARRIS.)* Sam, you know Isidore Witmark. He published my very first song.

ISIDORE WITMARK. More than twenty years ago!

GMC. I don't forget a thing.

ISIDORE WITMARK. *(Handing manuscript to GMC.)* Some friends of mine have written a musical. Could you read their script and let me know if it's as good as I think it is? It's an operetta set in a mythical European kingdom. You see, there's a handsome Prince who disguises himself as a commoner ...

GMC. ... and he falls in love with a beautiful but humble commoner who has no idea he's royalty.... Izzy, out of respect for you, I'll read it. Can't wait. *(WITMARK exits downstage left. Confiding to audience out of the corner of his mouth.)* It was the single worst script I'd ever seen. The kind of show that *my* shows had made obsolete. I made a decision at once. *(GMC crosses over to SAM HARRIS and thumps him on his chest with the back of hand.)* Sam! Send a wire to our friend Isidore Witmark:

> "Dear Izzy: Have never read anything quite like this script. Stop. Am buying all rights. Stop. Sam and I will put the show into production at once, to open June 15th at the Cohan and Harris Theatre on 42nd Street. Stop. Yankee Doodlefully Yours--George M."

(GMC exits into wings stage right.)

SAM HARRIS. *(To audience.)* In the next six days, George applied his pencil to the script. He worked in praise for American-style democracy. He crafted six new songs. And he transformed the show, "The Royal Vagabond," into a burlesque of old-style European operettas. Audiences packed the Cohan and Harris Theater. Everyone—except maybe poor Isidore Witmark—was delighted.

(GMC and AGNES NOLAN enter from upstage right. They are wearing gold crowns and they are holding hands.
Song: GMC and AGNES NOLAN sing the first few lines of the refrain of "IN A KINGDOM OF OUR OWN.")

GMC. *(Sings:)*
IN A KINGDOM OF OUR OWN,
WITH LITTLE CUPID ON THE THRONE,
   AGNES NOLAN. *(Sings:)*
WITH A PRINCE AND PRINCESS ON MY KNEE;
YOU'LL BE AS HAPPY AS A KING CAN BE ...

(GMC and AGNES NOLAN step apart. GMC lets go of AGNES NOLAN's hand reluctantly. AGNES NOLAN exits upstage left. GMC removes his crown.
WITMARK enters from downstage left.)

ISIDORE WITMARK. *(To GMC, agitated.)* You've taken a perfectly good script I gave you, and you've—you've—you've *Cohanized* it! You've changed every single line. And you're still waving that American flag!

GMC. That's just the kind of a little guy I am.

(GMC hands his crown to the nonplussed WITMARK, who exits downstage left.)

SAM HARRIS. *(To audience.)* We were flooded with scripts from other writers, asking George to please Cohanize their works, too.

GMC. *(To audience.)* I did what I could.

SAM HARRIS. *(To audience.)* The press, over time, came to treat George more seriously.

(Two REPORTERS enter from upstage right slot, carrying pads, ready to take notes. They stand a bit upstage of GMC as they ask him questions.)

REPORTER #1. *(To GMC.)* Mr. Cohan, in your latest play you say: "The Senate is a body of men surrounded by Standard Oil." Do you really believe the oil industry has too much influence?

GMC. Now, now. If I can be serious for just a moment.... I believe the United States Senate is the finest body of men that money

can buy.
REPORTER #2. Honest?
GMC. No, senators.
REPORTER #1. In your shows, you've taken jabs at senators and congressmen—
GMC. — who, I must admit, often do work rather hard for the corporations they represent.... But what do I know? Didn't Walter Pritchard Eaton of *The Tribune* just write, "The problem with Cohan is he has no idea how things work in the real world?" ... Truthfully, boys, I think loving your country sometimes means talking about what's wrong with your country, and trying to make it right. Next question....

(Song: MEMBERS OF THE ENSEMBLE march onstage briskly singing or chanting one chorus of "F-A-M-E." The reporters join in with them, becoming part of the chorus.)

MEMBERS OF THE ENSEMBLE. *(Sing:)*
FAME, FAME, FAME, FAME,
EV'RY ONE TRIES TO BEAT THE GAME,
TO MAKE A NAME, IT IS THE AIM
OF EV'RY MAN AND CHILD AND DAME,
FAME, FAME, FAME, FAME.
EVER THE SAME SO WHO'S TO BLAME,
THE GREAT WERE TAME UNTIL THEY CAME
TO F-A-M-E,
FAME, FAME, FAME.

(Upon hitting the last word, the MEMBERS OF THE ENSEMBLE stop and pivot, so they are in a line, facing upstage. They stand still, forming a kind of backdrop upstage of GMC and SAM.)

SAM HARRIS. *(To GMC.)* You and me ... in all those years, we never argued.
GMC. *(To SAM HARRIS)* Except when you'd try to book one of my shows into Poughkeepsie. And I'd have to remind you how they threw rocks at me there. And potatoes.
SAM HARRIS. *(To GMC.)* George, that was back when you were *thirteen*! *(To audience.)* He wouldn't change his mind about Poughkeepsie.
GMC. *(To audience.)* I did finally go back to Providence,

though. I wanted to thank a musician, Josh Brock, who'd been kind to me at a time when I needed kindness.

SAM HARRIS. *(To audience.)* George treated a hundred Providence musicians to a banquet that night. A great crowd. Brock was guest of honor. *(The MEMBERS OF THE ENSEMBLE move into place to form an audience for GMC; they are now the guests at the banquet.)* George got up and entertained everyone.

(SAM HARRIS is part of the audience for GMC now.)

GMC. My friends, I've written a little number I'd like to share with you. And Josh—don't go telling me to take this song to Witmark! This song is just for tonight.

(Song: GMC sings—and dances a bit, in a break—"THEN I'D BE SATISFIED WITH LIFE." [An option—GMC could perform this number atop a table if desired; Cohan actually did get up and dance on the table at various occasions, including the real-life banquet that inspired this scene.])

GMC. *(Sings freely:)*
HOW SELDOM WILL YOU MEET A MAN AS THROUGH THIS
    WORLD YOU GO,
A MAN, I MEAN, WHO'S SATISFIED WITH LIFE.
HE MAY BE BLESSED WITH WEALTH BUT WHERE'S HIS
    HEALTH? DON'T YOU KNOW,
HIS FIGHT FOR MILLIONS BRINGS HIM CARE AND STRIFE.
THE KING BOTH GREAT AND GRAND WHO HAS A LAND AT
    HIS COMMAND
WILL WANT HIS FLAG TO REACH ANOTHER SHORE.
AH THIS LIFE WE LEAD IS GREED,
THOUGH THERE ARE SOME THINGS I NEED.
IF I HAD THEM I WOULD ASK FOR NOTHING MORE.

(Insouciantly:)
ALL I WANT IS FIFTY MILLION DOLLARS
AND SEALSKINS TO PROTECT ME FROM THE COLD.
IF I ONLY KNEW HOW STOCKS WOULD GO IN WALL STREET,
AND WAS LIVING IN A MANSION BUILT OF GOLD.
IF THE VANDERBILTS WOULD LET ME SPEND THEIR
    MONEY.

IF I ONLY HAD AN HEIRESS FOR A WIFE ...
(Spoken aside; this should be slipped in without losing a beat.)
—I'd settle for a chorus girl!

(Sings :)
IF I ONLY STOOD IN WITH THE STEEL-TRUST RAKE-OFF,
THEN I KNOW THAT I'D BE SATISFIED WITH LIFE.

ALL I WANT IS PARTRIDGE FOR MY BREAKFAST,
A CHAMPAGNE FOUNTAIN SPRINKLING AT MY FEET.
PIERPONT MORGAN WAITING ON THE TABLE
AND SOUSA'S BAND PLAYING WHILE I EAT....

(The piano plays the next two lines of the refrain while GMC simply dances a bit, soft-shoe, not singing.... Then he resumes singing to conclude the song.)
IF I ONLY OWNED THE PENNSYLVANIA RAILROAD,
THEN I KNOW THAT I'D BE SATISFIED WITH ...
(Spoken interjection:) Isn't that a pretty song?

(The MEMBERS OF THE ENSEMBLE pantomime stylized applause and exit. Only GMC and SAM HARRIS remain onstage.)

SAM HARRIS. *(To audience.)* I never saw George happier than he was that night.
GMC. *(To audience.)* Singing, dancing, saying "thank you"— they're good for the soul.
SAM HARRIS. *(To audience.)* In the mean time, while performing eight shows a week in "The Honeymooners," George wrote and composed another musical with a star part for himself. It was called "Fifty Miles from Boston." *(George's DOCTOR enters from the wings stage right, holding a clipboard with papers.)* George's doctor told him:
DOCTOR. You're driving yourself too hard, you need more rest. The first thing you'll lose will be your voice.
GMC. Listen, I don't care if I lose my voice. Nobody will know the difference.

(The DOCTOR exits downstage left.)

SAM HARRIS *(To audience.)* When the losses started coming, they were not what he expected. Josie had never gotten along with George's wife, Ethel Levey.

(JOSIE steps out from the wings stage right. A suitcase is in her hand.)

JOSIE. *(To GMC.)* I'm marrying Fred Niblo.
GMC. Well, Josie.... Fred strikes me as a rather promising actor. I'll make sure he always has a job in the Cohan organization.
JOSIE. Actually, Fred and I are thinking of going off on tour by ourselves. And wherever he wants to go, I'll go.

(JOSIE exits into wings stage right.)

GMC. *(To audience.)* I couldn't believe Josie would walk out. In my next play, I named one of the characters "Josie," so she was at least symbolically still with us. I kept hoping she'd return to the fold. She and Fred found work in Australia.

(Song: MEMBERS OF THE ENSEMBLE enter from upstage left, and sing or chant another chorus of "F-A-M-E" while moving across the stage to exit into the wings stage right. But the tempo is slower, the mood is darker, the voices are quieter now.)

THE ENSEMBLE. *(Sings:)*
FAME, FAME, FAME, FAME,
HUSTLE UNTIL WE'RE OLD AND LAME,
WE'RE ALL THE SAME, WE'RE IN THE GAME,
TO GET OUR PICTURES IN A FRAME.
FAME, FAME, FAME, FAME,
NEVER A CHANCE WITHOUT A NAME,
IT SEEMS A SHAME, THE ONLY AIM
IS F-A-M-E,
FAME, FAME, FAME.

(The MEMBERS OF THE ENSEMBLE exit into the wings stage right. GMC exits with them.)

SAM HARRIS. *(To audience.)* Ethel Levey filed for divorce, charging George with infidelity. She divorced him and moved to England. George didn't understand how she could leave New York

City—*Broadway*—much less him. For him, anything outside of Manhattan was the sticks.

(ETHEL LEVEY enters from upstage right and moves towards the center.)

ETHEL. *(To SAM HARRIS.)* Can't I speak for myself? Don't I deserve even a single line of dialogue? *(SAM HARRIS makes a gesture, as if yielding the floor to her, and exits upstage left; ETHEL LEVEY speaks to the audience.)* I was not a nobody. I played the female lead in "Little Johnny Jones." I earned a good living. When I divorced George, he generously offered me $100,000. I told him I did not need money. After the divorce, I moved to England and for many years was a star there, in vaudeville and musical comedy.

When George eventually got around to writing his autobiography—he completed it in three weeks—he never so much as mentioned me, or the child I bore him. He never mentioned his second wife, either, or the three children that she bore him. But he certainly mentioned his father and mother, and sister Josie, and Sam Harris plenty. And already he could say:

(ETHEL LEVEY moves back. GMC enters from upstage left slot.)

GMC. *(To audience.)* In twenty years I have written, signed, and produced 31 plays of my own.

In addition, I have collaborated with other authors on 14 plays.

I've written and composed 500 songs and musical numbers.

I have produced, owned, controlled 128 theatrical attractions.

I have personally appeared in my own plays 428 weeks, 3,471 performances. That's not counting at least 200 testimonials and benefits.

The real answer is work, work, and lots of it—and plenty of speed, too, kid. Don't forget the speed.

(GMC exits upstage right.)

ETHEL. *(To audience.)* In my divorce papers, I did allege there was another woman in George's life. I might have been able to compete if there'd *only* been another woman. But I could not compete for his attention with the show business. And I could never have really become one of the Four Cohans. I remember a rehearsal when

George sharply criticized the performance of his father, who was getting forgetful. For a week, the tension was unbearable. It only broke the night I entered George's dressing room and found him seated on his mother's lap, crying, while she consoled him the way you'd console a child.... I always liked George; how could you not? There's so much more I want to say but—

(SAM HARRIS enters from upstage left, moves down.)

SAM HARRIS. *(To audience, cutting ETHEL off.)* But, but to be honest—the female characters were usually sketchily drawn in George's shows. *(GMC enters from downstage left.)* The one character portrayed most vividly tended be an insouciant young man ... not unlike George M. himself. Even after their divorce, Ethel continued performing Cohan songs. George liked that. And when George was hurt in an out-of-state car accident, *both* of his wives made their way to the hospital to show support.

(Song excerpt: "I WANT YOU." ETHEL LEVEY exits, heading upstage left, plaintively singing—either with soft piano accompaniment or a capella—the beginning of the chorus of "I Want You ...")

ETHEL LEVEY. *(Sings:)*
I WANT YOU,
YES I DO.
YOU, JUST YOU, YOU.
CAN'T YOU UNDERSTAND ME?
I DON'T CARE ABOUT
THE PRESENTS THAT YOU HAND ME.
I'M SO BLUE,
LONELY TOO....

(AGNES NOLAN enters from upstage right, walking towards GMC with the look of someone in love.)

SAM HARRIS. *(To audience.)* Four months after the divorce from Ethel, George married Agnes Nolan, who'd been in the chorus of "Little Johnny Jones."

(Song excerpt: "I WANT YOU." AGNES and GMC, gazing romantically at one another, sing the end of the chorus, finishing

the song ETHEL had begun.)

AGNES and GMC. *(Sing:)*
... I DON'T WANT YOUR MONEY, HONEY,
I WANT YOU.

SAM HARRIS. *(To audience.)* I then married Agnes Nolan's sister, Alice Nolan, who'd likewise been in that chorus. *(ALICE NOLAN enters from downstage left, taking her place at SAM's side.)* We got married in the same Freehold, New Jersey, courthouse where George had gotten married. And I built a home next door to George. So George was not only my closest friend and business partner, he was my brother-in-law.

(AGNES NOLAN crosses down to center.)

AGNES. *(To audience.)* I was one of eighteen brothers and sisters. President Theodore Roosevelt gave my father a medal for having the most children of any man in Massachusetts. George practically adopted the whole clan. He bought us a summer compound up in Massachusetts. Across from us, there was another fellow with the same idea for his clan: Joseph Kennedy.

SAM HARRIS. *(To audience.)* There was always another show, another song to pour his energies into. He soon came up with a number I particularly liked—a spoof, which most audience members took seriously, even with an introduction like this.

(SAM HARRIS and his wife exit downstage right.)

AGNES. *(With exaggerated theatricality.)* I'm leaving New York City. I'm leaving New York for good. I yearn for the tranquility of beautiful Buffalo. There I'll settle down and make my future ... along the Erie Canal.

(Song: "DOWN BY THE ERIE.")

AGNES. *(Sings:)*
IF YOU WANT TO MAKE GOOD IN A BROADWAY SHOW,
YOU MUST HAVE A SONG THAT IS SURE TO GO,
A PRETTY LITTLE DITTY
THAT THEY WHISTLE 'ROUND THE CITY,

AND THEY PLAY EV'RYWHERE,
EV'RY DAY EV'RYWHERE;
IT'S A REGULAR, POPULAR TIN PAN SONG,
THE KIND OF A MELODY CAN'T GO WRONG;
A CATCHY REFRAIN, THE SORT OF A STRAIN
THAT GIVES YOU A PAIN
WHEN YOU HEAR IT AGAIN.
THE ORCHESTRA MURDERS IT O'ER AND O'ER,
THE USHERS APPLAUD AND THEY SHOUT FOR MORE,
THEY RESORT TO THE TRICK
OF THE GALLERY "CLIQUE"
SO THE ENCORES WILL NOT MISS.
THE MANAGEMENT FEATURES IT NEAR AND FAR.
IT'S USUALLY SUNG BY THE FEMALE STAR.
THE PUBLISHER GIVES HER A MOTOR CAR.
AND THE CHORUS GOES SOMETHING LIKE THIS.

(Spoken interjection to the piano player, as if ordering the tempo she wants for the refrain.) Six-seven-eight! *(Sings:)*

DOWN BY THE ERIE,
THERE WAITS MY PAL;
THOUGH THE DAYS ARE LONG AND DREARY,
HE DECLARES HE'LL NE'ER GROW WEARY.
POOR JOHN O'LEARY,
I'M AFRAID YOU'VE LOST YOUR GAL.
FOR I'VE LEFT YOU FLAT, MY DEARIE,
BY THE ERIE CANAL.

(SAM HARRIS enters from wings, stage right.)

SAM HARRIS. *(To audience; as he speaks AGNES NOLAN walks slowly upstage left to exit; she is gone by the end of his talk about her.)* Agnes retired from the stage to raise their children. Someone had to do it, and George wasn't cut out to be a parent. Agnes suffered health problems, eventually becoming an invalid. George's occasional affairs were discreet. The shows and songs kept coming.

(SAM HARRIS exits into wings, stage right.
GMC enters from upstage right.
Song: "I WANT TO HEAR A YANKEE DOODLE TUNE.")

GMC. *(Sings, with spirit:)*
I'VE ALWAYS HATED
THIS OVER-RATED,
PRETENTIOUS MUSIC, COMPLICATED,
AND COMPOSITIONS
THAT HAVE CONDITIONS,
AND INTERMISSIONS THAT PLEASE MUSICIANS.
IT'S HARD TO HEAR IT, OR JUST BE NEAR IT.
UPON MY WORD I ALWAYS FEAR IT,
FOR I'M THE ORIGINAL CRANKY, YANKEE POPULAR
    MELODY FOOL.

GIVE ME A TUNE THAT'S WORTH A-LISTENING
GIVE ME A TUNE THAT'S WORTH A-WHISTLING.
I WANT A SOUSA STRAIN
INSTEAD OF A WAGNER PAIN.
GIVE THE TROMBONE A CHANCE TO BLOW IN IT,
GIVE ME DASH OF RAG AND GO IN IT.
WHAT I'M STATING
IS ADVOCATING
THE POPULAR MELODY SCHOOL.

I WANT TO HEAR A YANKEE DOODLE TUNE,
PLAYED BY A MILITARY BAND.
I WANT TO HEAR A YANKEE DOODLE TUNE,
THE ONLY MUSIC I CAN UNDERSTAND.
OH! SOUSA, WON'T YOU WRITE ANOTHER MARCH.
YOURS IS JUST THE MELODY DIVINE.
YOU MAY HAVE YOUR WILLIAM TELL,
AND FAUST AND LOHENGRIN AS WELL,
BUT I'LL TAKE A YANKEE DOODLE TUNE FOR MINE.

GIVE ME THE FELLOW
WHO WRITES THE MELLOW
CONTAGIOUS STRAIN THAT'S RATHER YELLOW.
IT MAY BE HASHY,
AND MAY BE TRASHY,
BUT STILL IT'S DASHY AND GETS THE CASHY.
IT'S REALLY CLEVER
AND LASTS FOREVER.
YOU HEAR IT ONCE, FORGET IT NEVER.

FOR NOW WE ARE COMING TO HANKY-PANKY, POPULAR
    MELODY DAYS.
THAT IT'S THE MUSIC, THERE'S NO DOUBT OF IT.
CUT ALL THE CHEAP CADENZAS OUT OF IT.
MUSIC TO PLEASE THE GANG
WITH PLENTY OF BIFF AND BANG;
MUSIC THAT ALL THE CHILDREN HUM A BIT,
ALL THE COMPOSER'S GLORIES COME OF IT.
IT'S SO RINGING,
THAT'S WHAT IS BRINGING
THE POPULAR MELODY CRAZE.

I WANT TO HEAR A YANKEE DOODLE TUNE,
PLAYED BY A MILITARY BAND.
I WANT TO HEAR A YANKEE DOODLE TUNE,
THE ONLY MUSIC I CAN UNDERSTAND.
OH! SOUSA, WON'T YOU WRITE ANOTHER MARCH.
YOURS IS JUST THE MELODY DIVINE.
YOU MAY HAVE YOUR WILLIAM TELL,
AND FAUST AND LOHENGRIN AS WELL,
BUT I'LL TAKE A YANKEE DOODLE TUNE FOR MINE.

(GMC exits. SAM HARRIS enters from wings stage right.)

SAM HARRIS. *(To audience.)* We were a theatrical empire. George was prolific, and never worried about how things *usually* were done. He'd put shows into rehearsal when he'd written as little as one scene, and build the rest as he went along. He wrote one musical where he never got around to the first song until Act Two. And another musical with a plot so slight he put in a song bragging we had no plot. He wrote one show without an intermission, and another where—instead of a set—the theater itself was the set; you saw the actual back wall of the theater. All of that was novel.

(Director JULIAN MITCHELL and CHORUS GIRLS begin quietly filing onstage while SAM is giving the speech above. A young actor, PERCY, brings out a chair for MITCHELL so he can sit and supervise the CHORUS GIRLS, while facing stage left. The actor playing MITCHELL pantomimes, signaling where to set the chair down, while HARRIS is giving the above speech. This business of entering and getting ready should be timed so that as

HARRIS finishes the above speech, MITCHELL is seated, ready to begin the next scene.)

JULIAN MITCHELL. *(To the CHORUS GIRLS.)* All right, girls. *(To the pianist.)* Harvey, are you ready now? Five, six, seven, eight. *(The pianist begins softly playing the refrain of "Harrigan" while the girls dance soft-shoe to it at stage left.)* Very nice, very nice. ... *(After perhaps six or so bars of music, GMC enters from the upstage right slot to observe the rehearsal. When the dancers and the pianist notice that GMC has arrived, the dancers, one by one, stop dancing, and the pianist stops playing. GMC has his jacket off, and is carrying a pair of dancing shoes. JULIAN MITCHELL, with his back to GMC, isn't aware that GMC has entered the room and doesn't understand why the dancers and the pianist have stopped.)* Girls! Girls! Why have you stopped dancing?

CLARISSE (A Chorus Girl). Excuse me, Julian, but Mr. Cohan has just come in.

JULIAN MITCHELL. *(With exaggerated dignity.)* My dear, it is "Julian" in bed. It is "Mr. Mitchell" in the theater.

GMC. Well, how is our rehearsal going? I was watching a bit from the back of the house. Clarisse, it looks like you still haven't mastered your lines yet.

CLARISSE. I just don't understand it, Mr. Cohan. I knew my lines perfectly last night in bed.

GMC. Props! One bed!

(Everyone laughs. One of the chorus gals touches GMC lightly, possessively, by the elbow, suggesting some intimacy.)

JULIAN MITCHELL. George, we've got a more serious problem. Donald Brian quit the cast today—he's been offered a chance to star in a Schubert operetta.

SAM HARRIS. He'll never work for us again!

GMC. Not unless we need him! He dances great.

JULIAN MITCHELL. George, our problem isn't just that we've lost Donald. His understudy can't cut it. I've had to let him go. We've got no one.

(GMC looks around till he sees a young chorus member standing stage right; he hands off his tap shoes to SAM HARRIS to hold, and crosses over to the young chorus member.)

GMC. Percy! Percy Helton! You're the youngest member of our company. But I knew your father. And I know your potential. You're a trouper like he was. Could you handle Donald's part?

PERCY. I don't know. I don't think so. Maybe.

(GMC slaps the kid! It is a sharp stage slap, catching everyone by surprise. The dancers gasp. PERCY holds his hand to his face where he's been slapped. Then GMC hugs him and says emphatically:)

GMC. You're in the theater, Perce. And I know you're going to stay in the theater. And *if* a director, *if* a producer, *if* an author asks if you can do something—I don't care if he asks if you can play Shylock in *The Merchant of Venice*—you tell him *Yes*. My father taught me that when I was ten. Now can you do the part?

PERCY. *(Nervously.) Yes*, Mr. Cohan!

GMC. Atta boy! *(GMC and PERCY move downstage.)* I know it's hard for you. But the good times are just ahead. *(GMC takes some sheet music from the top of the piano, gives it to the pianist and tells PERCY:)* Now follow me!

(Song: GMC teaches PERCY ""HARRIGAN" and they both sing/dance it. The first verse and chorus will be sung, then there will be an instrumental chorus—over which GMC and PERCY will speak to one another, while they continue moving about to the music—then they will sing another verse and chorus. PERCY is clearly uncertain at the start of this number, gradually gaining confidence in his performance. PERCY has little to do at first beyond piping up to sing the words "Harrigan, that's me," while GMC sings the verse. By the time they finish the number, though, they are moving about the stage with surety, singing and dancing—not tap dancing, just moving around the stage with style together—like a good team.)

GMC. *(Sings:)*
WHO IS THE MAN WHO WILL SPEND OR WILL EVEN LEND?
PERCY. *(Sings, shyly, nervously:)*
HARRIGAN, THAT'S ME!
GMC. *(Sings:)*
WHO IS YOUR FRIEND WHEN YOU FIND THAT YOU NEED A FRIEND?

PERCY. *(Sings:)*
HARRIGAN, THAT'S ME!

GMC. *(Sings:)*
FOR I'M JUST AS PROUD OF MY NAME, YOU SEE,
AS AN EMPEROR, CZAR, OR A KING, COULD BE.

(The music corresponding to the above line is repeated and GMC does a jig to it, and then continues singing the song.)

WHO IS THE MAN HELPS A MAN EV'RY TIME HE CAN?
    PERCY. *(Sings:)*
HARRIGAN, THAT'S ME!

    GMC and PERCY. *(Sing together:)*
H - A - DOUBLE R - I - G - A - N SPELLS HARRIGAN,
PROUD OF ALL THE IRISH BLOOD THAT'S IN ME;
DIVIL A MAN CAN SAY A WORD AGIN ME.
H - A - DOUBLE R - I - G - A - N, YOU SEE,
IS A NAME THAT A SHAME NEVER HAS BEEN CONNECTED
    WITH.
HARRIGAN, THAT'S ME!

    GMC. *(To PERCY while teaching him "Harrigan." These are lines to be spoken after the first chorus has been sung, while just moving about to the instrumental chorus, before singing the final verse and chorus.)* Roam the stage like it belongs to you, Perce. Own it! Do you know, when I was starting out, dancers often stayed in one spot? I changed that.
    PERCY. I know, Mr. Cohan. I was eight the first time I saw you run across the stage and flip off of the proscenium arch. My dad said, "If you ever try that, Percy, I'll murder you!"
    GMC. Ha-hah! You ever need help with anything, young man, you ask for it. Now, sing like you mean it!

(They finish the song.)

    GMC. *(Sings:)*
WHO IS THE MAN NEVER STOOD FOR A GADABOUT?
    PERCY. *(Sings:)*
HARRIGAN, THAT'S ME!

GMC. *(Sings:)*
WHO IS THE MAN THAT THE TOWN'S SIMPLY MAD ABOUT?
PERCY. *(Sings:)*
HARRIGAN, THAT'S ME!

THE LADIES AND BABIES ARE FOND OF ME,
I'M FOND OF THEM, TOO, IN RETURN, YOU SEE.

(The music corresponding to the above line is repeated; PERCY does a jig to it and then continues singing the song.)

WHO IS THE GENT THAT'S DESERVING A MONUMENT?
HARRIGAN, THAT'S ME!

GMC and PERCY. *(Sing together:)*
H - A - DOUBLE R - I - G - A - N SPELLS HARRIGAN,
PROUD OF ALL THE IRISH BLOOD THAT'S IN ME;
DIVIL A MAN CAN SAY A WORD AGIN ME.
H - A - DOUBLE R - I - G - A - N, YOU SEE,
IS A NAME THAT A SHAME NEVER HAS BEEN CONNECTED
  WITH.
HARRIGAN, THAT'S ME!

GMC. You've got the goods, Perce. I'll have you running up the proscenium arch before long. *Think* about the theater when you leave here. And pay special attention to that monologue you've got in Act Two, the one that begins: "There's no happiness for people of the theater, outside the theater—take it from me...."

PERCY. *(To audience, while everyone else on stage is frozen, unaware.)* I was proud to do shows with George M. Cohan. A wonderful man. He taught me a lot. He helped launch my career, as he did for so many others, from Walter Huston to Spencer Tracy. And we adored him.

He'd tell us we were like family to him. I sometimes wondered, though, how much time he had for his own family—his wife and children.

I'm not sure if any of us who worked with Mr. Cohan ever really knew the man. Some of the actors would say, "The Little Fellow"— that's what they'd call him—they'd say, "The Little Fellow is a mystery." He rarely volunteered much about himself, except to reminisce in a sweet, sometimes sad, way about his youth in the Four

Cohans.

I sure remember his kindness, though, and his puckish charm. I remember the night we left the theater in a downpour. Without saying a word, he draped his coat over my shoulders and insisted I take the first cab, not he. I can't imagine any of the stars I worked with in later years doing that for a young unknown. But his life, I somehow felt—his real life—was up there on the stage.

(PERCY exits into wings stage right. JULIAN MITCHELL and SAM HARRIS exit upstage left. On his way out, JULIAN moves the chair from center stage to a position stage left—almost to the edge of the stage—so it is out of the way for the dance scene coming up. And SAM HARRIS sets GMC's tap shoes by the chair.)

GMC. *(To cast.)* Now let's run through this dance number. It's a little ragtime march I've written called "Popularity." Give it all you've got. Five-six-seven-eight.

CELESTE. Excuse me, Mr. Cohan, in my next scene what is my motivation?

GMC. My dear Celeste, you'll find out your motivation on opening night.

(Musical number: "POPULARITY." This ragtime march is a dance number but not a tap dance number. This instrumental piece will be played as originally written by Cohan—omitting, however, the repeats. GMC and the CHORUS GIRLS start dancing. During the number, JERRY and NELLIE COHAN—coming out from the wings stage right—join the proceedings, so we see three COHANS dancing with and then in front of the others in the cast. At the end, JERRY and NELLIE COHAN are obviously winded. Everyone exits the stage except for JERRY, NELLIE and GMC.)

GMC. *(To his parents.)* You catch your breath. You've got to save something for opening night.

JERRY. And it will be our last opening night. It's been a long run, son. Mother and I have had all the fun in the world, but one has got to learn how to bow out and when to bow out, and for us, this is it.

GMC. You can't quit. Why, I've been giving the same curtain speech for over twenty-five years: 'My father thanks you, my mother thanks you ....' *(To audience.)* For his 66th birthday, I made my father my equal partner in all Cohan enterprises, sharing in all income from my songs, my shows, my theaters ....

JERRY. I could never read that letter without weeping. That son was a gift to us.

When Nellie and I retired in 1914, George announced that he was retiring from performing, along with us. He said he would concentrate on raising his own children. He felt so close to us, he could not imagine going forward without us.

The creative urge was too strong, of course, for him to stay out for long. Within ten months, he was once again starring on Broadway.

(JERRY and NELLIE exit quietly upstage left.)

GMC. *(To audience.)* In 1916, my sister Josie died. Doctors said she had a bad heart, weakened by overwork as a performer. To me, her husband Fred Niblo was the man who took her away from us. *(The REPORTER enters from the wings, stage right.)* And when that one reporter I liked, who simply didn't know better, asked:

REPORTER. What do you think of Fred Niblo's work?

GMC. *(To audience.)* I told him frankly: *(To REPORTER.)* Fred Niblo? If you don't mind, Ward, that's a name we don't mention around here. *(The REPORTER exits into the wings stage right. To audience.)*

I bought a mausoleum for the family, in Woodhaven Cemetery in the Bronx. The Four Cohans would be reunited there, someday. Sam Harris took a plot close by.

The year after Josie died, my father died. I went on the only period of hard, sustained drinking in my life.

Do you believe in ghosts? In spirits? Until my father died, I never did. He did—but I wrote it off as Old World superstition. The first time I heard his cough in the theater, after he died, I said my grieving, anxious mind was playing tricks on me. But in years to come I saw him, and my late sister and mother, as well. I knew they were there in the theater with me. They often were. If you've come to commune with Cohan spirits, you're in the right neighborhood.

(Lights dim and come up. Entering from the wings stage right, a CHORUS GAL changes the vaudeville placard as GMC watches. She removes and carries offstage the placard that says "The Four Cohans," so that we now see a placard reading, "Mr. Cohan, Alone."

GEORGE M. COHAN: IN HIS OWN WORDS

Song: "LIFE'S A FUNNY PROPOSITION AFTER ALL." This poignant Cohan rarity—a ballad essentially unheard for nearly a century, and a major rediscovery--is a key number of the show. A reflection on life and death, it provides a dramatic turning point, setting a subdued mood for the play's final stretch, from the George's father's death to his own. GMC pulls the chair into position—a bit more onstage. He sits down on the chair, and begins changing out of his regular shoes into his tap shoes. And while seated and taking off his shoes, he begins to sing. This business of changing the shoes onstage is both practical—GMC is going to need to be in the tap shoes for the show's finale—and dramatically effective. He is quietly changing his clothes, reflecting on life. He should remain seated for about half the number, rising to give added impact for the second refrain.)

GMC. *(Sings reflectively.)*
DID YOU EVER SIT AND PONDER, SIT AND WONDER, SIT AND THINK,
WHY WE'RE HERE AND WHAT THIS LIFE IS ALL ABOUT?
IT'S A PROBLEM THAT HAS DRIVEN MANY BRAINY MEN TO DRINK.
IT'S THE WEIRDEST THING THEY'VE TRIED TO FIGURE OUT.
ABOUT A THOUSAND DIFF'RENT THEORIES ALL THE SCIENTISTS CAN SHOW,
BUT NEVER YET HAVE PROVED A REASON WHY
WITH ALL WE'VE THOUGHT AND ALL WE'RE TAUGHT, WHY ALL WE SEEM TO KNOW
IS WE'RE BORN AND LIVE A WHILE, AND THEN WE DIE.

LIFE'S A VERY FUNNY PROPOSITION AFTER ALL,
IMAGINATION, JEALOUSY, HYPOCRISY AND ALL.
THREE MEALS A DAY, A WHOLE LOT TO SAY.
WHEN YOU HAVEN'T GOT THE COIN YOU'RE ALWAYS IN THE WAY.
EV'RYBODY'S FIGHTING AS WE WEND OUR WAY ALONG.
EV'RY FELLOW CLAIMS THE OTHER FELLOW'S IN THE WRONG.
HURRIED AND WORRIED UNTIL WE'RE BURIED AND THERE'S NO CURTAIN CALL.
LIFE'S A VERY FUNNY PROPOSITION AFTER ALL.

WHEN ALL THINGS ARE COMING EASY, AND WHEN LUCK IS WITH A MAN,
WHY THEN LIFE TO HIM IS SUNSHINE EV'RYWHERE;
THEN THE FATES BLOW RATHER BREEZY AND THEY QUITE UPSET A PLAN;
THEN HE'LL CRY THAT LIFE'S A BURDEN HARD TO BEAR.
THOUGH TODAY MAY BE A DAY OF SMILES, TOMORROW'S STILL IN DOUBT,
AND WHAT BRINGS ME JOY MAY BRING YOU CARE AND WOE.
WE'RE BORN TO DIE, BUT DON'T KNOW WHY, OR WHAT IT'S ALL ABOUT,
AND THE MORE WE TRY TO LEARN THE LESS WE KNOW.

LIFE'S A VERY FUNNY PROPOSITION, YOU CAN BET,
AND NO ONE'S EVER SOLVED THE PROBLEM PROPERLY AS YET.
YOUNG FOR A DAY, THEN OLD AND GRAY.
LIKE THE ROSE THAT BUDS AND BLOOMS AND FADES AND FALLS AWAY,
LOSING HEALTH TO GAIN OUR WEALTH AS THRO' THIS DREAM WE TOUR.
EV'RYTHING'S A GUESS AND NOTHING'S ABSOLUTELY SURE;
BATTLES EXCITING AND FATES WE'RE FIGHTING UNTIL THE CURTAIN FALL,
LIFE'S A VERY FUNNY PROPOSITION AFTER ALL.

(To audience.) When my father died, I thought my life was over.

(SAM HARRIS enters.)

SAM HARRIS. *(To audience.)* His life was far from over. He had another quarter-century to go. By his last decade, he was widely recognized as America's pre-eminent stage actor. Critics called him "The First Actor."

GMC. *(To audience humbly.)* When you do something for sixty years, you learn a little about how to do it.

SAM HARRIS. *(To audience.)* George starred in "The Tavern," as effective an American farce as had ever been created. He wrote that play in three days. He triumphed in Eugene O'Neill's "Ah,

Wilderness!" When some reporter asked if O'Neill wasn't a bit highbrow, he answered:

GMC. *(To audience.)* O'Neill's regular. His father was a great trouper, and a pretty good friend of my father.

SAM HARRIS *(To audience.)* George was a legend. When he did "I'd Rather Be Right," he generated the biggest theatrical advance sale in nearly a decade. After the Broadway run, he toured the country until he was exhausted.

GMC. *(To audience.)* Pop always told me, "Never give up your dancing shoes." *(Getting an overcoat and hat from a coatrack at stage right, and putting them on.)* I worked simply.... As a dancer, I could never do over three steps. As a composer, I could never find use for over four or five notes in my musical numbers. I'm a one-key piano player, and as a playwright most of my plays have been presented in two acts for the simple reason that I could seldom think of an idea for the third act.

SAM HARRIS. *(To audience.)* He remained a loner. When actors banded to form Actor's Equity, he felt alienated, appalled at the notion of performers ever striking. He vowed he'd never join a union. Outside of family, he felt little need for banding in groups, or trusting in groups.

Equity could have insisted George sign their contracts like everyone else. But he'd simply initial a memorandum noting his salary and commitment to act "for the run of the play."

(GMC moves to get cane from coatrack. He seems older now; he moves a bit slower.)

GMC. *(To audience.)* I never much believed in contracts.

SAM HARRIS. *(To audience.)* He grew quieter, gentler, more like his father. And more distant, even from me. He didn't like to say much about the difficulties he had with his own family.

I remember lines George wrote for himself in "The Tavern," which struck me as being pretty close to the mark.

GMC. *(To audience.)* I don't know who I am. And if I did, I'd be the most miserable man on earth. For my greatest happiness lies in the fact that I occupy a most unique position—that of not having been cast for a part in the great world drama of life. I am the audience. In all the changing scenes of this ever-beginning, never-ending plotless plot, I recognize the spiritual hand of a great director, a master director who has so skillfully staged this tightly-knitted spectacle of tragic nonsense. And so I am amused, and I laugh, and I applaud.

SAM HARRIS. *(To audience.)* George was the first person in show business ever to be awarded a Congressional Medal of Honor. He took four years to get around to picking up his medal from President Roosevelt.

GMC. *(To audience.)* I wasn't a great believer in honors, publicly bestowed.

SAM HARRIS GMC. *(To audience.)* He turned down every University that proposed granting him an honorary degree.

GMC. I would have felt out of place, making a speech at a college. I never went to school. I said it many times: The theater is all I know--all I care to know. I loved my family, I loved the theater, I loved my country.

SAM HARRIS. *(To audience.)* He did head to Catholic University, however, in response to a letter from a young teacher there named Walter Kerr.

Kerr—who years later would become the theater critic of the New York Times—wrote George in 1939. He co-authored a campus musical about Cohan. The show charmed George, and inspired Warner Brothers to make a movie about him, "Yankee Doodle Dandy." As the film went into production, we were both terminally ill with cancer. I told him:

SAM HARRIS. *(Turning to GMC.)* My God, George, no actor ever did what you did in the theater. Doesn't that make you proud?

GMC. *(To SAM HARRIS, arm about HARRIS's shoulder.)* No complaints, kid, no complaints. *(GMC watches as HARRIS exits upstage left. To audience.)* The funny thing was, when that film went into production, my songs and sentiments were considered passé. "Over There" was a relic of the First World War.

By the time the film opened in 1942, however, we were immersed in the Second World War. My little song felt as relevant as ever.

Whenever this nation gets too complacent, too high-hat to wave a flag, we're given a reminder of just how hard-won our freedoms are, how vigilant we must remain.... *(GMC puts on a fedora, taken from the coatrack.)*

The last trip outside my home I ever took was against doctor's orders. I wanted to see Broadway one final time. *(As GMC, center-stage, speaks of pulling up his coat collar, pulling down his hat, etc., he acts it out.)*

Frail as I was, I pulled my coat collar up, and my hat brim down, so I wouldn't be recognized. I slipped into the theater, just off Times Square, where "Yankee Doodle Dandy" had opened. I watched James Cagney, playing myself, tell President Roosevelt: "Where else could a plain guy like me sit down and talk things over with the head man?" And heard the President, on screen, answer: "Well now, you know, Mr. Cohan, that's as good a definition of America as I've ever heard." I smiled a little. I'd actually written those lines for the picture.

I watched the ensemble sing "Over There" at the end, and went home to die. I'd given my regards to Broadway. That bit of "Yankee Doodle Dandy" was the last film I ever saw.

My daughter Georgette said, of that spirit-lifting movie, "That's the kind of a life Daddy would have liked to have led."

No complaints, kid. No complaints.

(Song: GMC sings softly as he heads upstage, with his back to us, the first two lines of the song "Always leave 'em laughing when you say goodbye." He does a flourish with the cane, done earlier in the same number by his father. He then turns to face the audience, singing softly but crisply, building in intensity: "OVER THERE." He is earnest, intent as he begins the verse: "Johnny get your gun ..." He sings the first verse and one chorus, alone on stage. Then the cast files on stage, entering from the upstage slots. The members of the ensemble start backing him in song, their mood—like his—at first solemn. Then it brightens.
He flings his hat to the wings. They all sing/dance "Over There" with gusto.)

GMC. *(Sings:)*
ALWAYS LEAVE 'EM LAUGHING WHEN YOU SAY
   GOODBYE.
NEVER LINGER LONG ABOUT OR ELSE YOU'LL WEAR
   YOUR WELCOME OUT ...

JOHNNIE GET YOUR GUN, GET YOUR GUN, GET YOUR GUN.
TAKE IT ON THE RUN, ON THE RUN, ON THE RUN.
HEAR THEM CALLING YOU AND ME,
EV'RY SON OF LIBERTY.
HURRY RIGHT AWAY, NO DELAY, GO TODAY.
MAKE YOUR DADDY GLAD TO HAVE HAD SUCH A LAD.
TELL YOUR SWEETHEART NOT TO PINE.
TO BE PROUD HER BOY'S IN LINE.

(At this point, the MEMBERS OF THE ENSEMBLE begin entering slowly. But they do not yet sing with GMC. He continues singing by himself.)
OVER THERE,
OVER THERE.
SEND THE WORD, SEND THE WORD, OVER THERE.
THAT THE YANKS ARE COMING,
THE YANKS ARE COMING.
THE DRUMS RUM-TUMMING EV'RYWHERE.
SO PREPARE,
SAY A PRAY'R.
SEND THE WORD, SEND THE WORD
TO BEWARE.
WE'LL BE OVER,
WE'RE COMING OVER.
AND WE WON'T COME BACK
TILL IT'S OVER OVER THERE.

GMC and ENTIRE ENSEMBLE. *(Sing:)*
OVER THERE,
OVER THERE.
SEND THE WORD, SEND THE WORD, OVER THERE.
THAT THE YANKS ARE COMING,
THE YANKS ARE COMING.
THE DRUMS RUM-TUMMING EV'RYWHERE.
SO PREPARE,
SAY A PRAY'R.
SEND THE WORD, SEND THE WORD
TO BEWARE.
WE'LL BE OVER,
WE'RE COMING OVER.
AND WE WON'T COME BACK
TILL IT'S OVER OVER THERE.

(The pianist begins playing the refrain again, for a double-time dance break. Everyone dances through one complete refrain, right through to the end of the refrain. Then Johnny and the ensemble start singing again.)

GMC and ENTIRE CAST. *(Sing:)*
SO PREPARE,

SAY A PRAY'R.
SEND THE WORD, SEND THE WORD
TO BEWARE.
WE'LL BE OVER,
WE'RE COMING OVER.
AND WE WON'T COME BACK
TILL IT'S OVER OVER THERE.

(The entire ensemble then goes into "YOU'RE A GRAND OLD FLAG" a capella. GMC is downstage center. While singing "You're a Grand Old Flag," the other cast members exit the stage one by one, touching GMC on the shoulder to say goodbye. They leave in the following order: MEMBERS OF THE ENSEMBLE, then SAM HARRIS, then finally Cohan's wives, then his sister, mother, and father. All touch him, his parents kiss him. He finishes the last line or so of the song by himself, alone on stage.)

THE ENSEMBLE. *(Sings slowly, poignantly:)*
YOU'RE A GRAND OLD FLAG,
YOU'RE A HIGH-FLYING FLAG.
AND FOREVER IN PEACE MAY YOU WAVE.
YOU'RE THE EMBLEM OF
THE LAND I LOVE,
THE HOME OF THE FREE AND THE BRAVE.
EV'RY HEART BEATS TRUE
UNDER RED, WHITE AND BLUE.
WHERE THERE'S NEVER A BOAST OR BRAG.

GMC. *(Sings:)*
"BUT SHOULD AULD ACQUAINTANCE BE FORGOT,"
KEEP YOUR EYE ON THE GRAND OLD FLAG.

(Blackout.
For the bows by the cast, the pianist plays "I Want to Hear a Yankee Doodle Tune," vamping as long as needed as the audience applauds. All the cast members get take their bows, and are exiting. Everything appears to be over, but then while the audience is still clapping, GMC looks at the audience as if he's thought of one more thing he needs to say, raises a hand as if to get their attention, and sings the last lines of the song, to

playfully put a button on the show.)

GMC. *(Sings:)*
You may have your William Tell,
And Faust and Lohengrin as well,
But I'll take a Yankee Doodle tune for mine.

(Blackout.)

THE END

COSTUMES

The show can be costumed as simply or as elaborately as you choose, with clothing evocative of the turn of the century.

Cohan lived from 1878-1942. Most events depicted in the play took place between approximately 1888 (when George would have been a 10-year-old with the Four Cohans) and 1917 (the year his father died, which was also the year that George wrote "Over There," the latest song in in this show). After trouping for years with the Four Cohans, George became a star on his own with the Broadway hit "Little Johnny Jones" in 1904. "Forty-Five Minutes" from Broadway followed in 1905, "The Yankee Prince" in 1907, etc. Costumes for *George M. Cohan: In His Own Words* should be suggestive of that era.

For the original New York production we chose to costume the show simply, but effectively, in the following manner.

We opted for a basic color scheme of dark blue and white, with occasional red accents (the red might turn up in a tie, a handkerchief, a sash, etc.). The basic outfit for female members of the ensemble was a dark blue or Navy skirt (at least mid-calf in length) and a white blouse, with a period feel. The basic outfit for the male members of the ensemble consisted of dark blue or Navy trousers and a white dress shirt. In musical numbers such as "The Man Who Owns Broadway," "I'm a Yankee Doodle Dandy" and "Over There," we chose to have ensemble members dressed rather uniformly, and Cohan, in front of them, costumed differently from them to stand out from the ensemble.

Principals got to dress more elaborately, as needed, for specific scenes—either wearing different outfits altogether, or using accessories to create different looks. For example, if the actress playing Ethel Levey was just supposed to be a member of the ensemble backing Cohan for a number, in that scene she wore the basic dark blue skirt/white blouse combination like every other chorus member. But in the scene where Ethel Levey performed her featured musical number, "The Warmest Baby in the Bunch," she wore a fancy, brocaded gown of the sort that a turn-of-the-century vaudeville headliner might wear (the gown we picked for her happened to be emerald green, but no specific color is required); when putting over that song, the performer has to look like a vaudeville *star*, not like some anonymous chorus girl. And we had Ethel Levey wear that same "star outfit" for the scene in which she gave her big monolog about divorcing Cohan.

The actress playing Agnes Nolan wore the basic blue and white outfit when appearing as just a member of the ensemble. But she added a striking red sash and shawl to create a much more star-like look when it came time for her to be introduced to audience as the former chorus girl who's marrying Cohan, and to sing, "Down by the Erie Canal."

George M. Cohan had three basic outfits in our original production. (He could certainly have additional changes of clothes, if desired, but three basic outfits are essential.) In the first scene (set in 1907), singing "You're a Grand Old Flag," he wears an old-style Army uniform, complete with cap, a dark blue jacket with buttons up the front, and a belt with a buckle. After that number, he changes (behind a folding screen onstage) into a dapper suit. For our production, this costume change was simply a matter of removing the Army jacket, belt, and cap, and putting on a suit jacket and a tie. We used the same pants (held up by suspenders) for both the dapper blue/gray suit and the Army outfit. For the suit, we gave Cohan a light blue dress shirt with discreet red and white stripes, plus a tie subtly using red and blue. The main thing was that he looked sharp—very natty. He performed much of the show wearing this suit. Sometimes in the show—like in the scene when he's supposed to be overseeing a rehearsal—he appeared without the jacket, perhaps rolling up his shirt sleeves. Near the very end of the show (as we approached Cohan's death in 1942), Cohan put on a fedora and an overcoat (a trench coat is fine), and used a cane.

For the "I'm a Yankee Doodle Dandy"/"Give My Regards to Broadway' scene which closes the first act, we had Cohan dressed as a jockey, with authentic white jockey pants, a white shirt, and a bold red vest. (With the rest of the cast dressed in dark blue and white, Cohan's splash of red helped draw attention to him.) The actor playing Cohan was actually wearing the jockey pants underneath his suit pants from the beginning of the play, so he could quickly make the costume change (from the dapper suit to the jockey outfit) in the wings—a time-saving option to consider.

For the scene where an excerpt of "In a Kingdom of Our Own" is sung, Cohan and Agnes Nolan should wear gold crowns, suggesting they are in a show playing royalty. If desired, they could also be wearing regal capes, or holding scepters.

For the scenes of the Four Cohans performing, we wanted to give

GEORGE M. COHAN: IN HIS OWN WORDS

the family some stylistic togetherness. So we had Nellie and Josie Cohan wearing somewhat similar outfits, and Jerry Cohan and George M. Cohan wearing somewhat similar outfits (with matching period garters on their upper shirt sleeves). A red bow tie gave Jerry a touch of color onstage. For the "Popularity: A Ragtime March" number, we had Nellie Cohan wear a feather boa. Nellie and Josie wore period wigs throughout. Josie sometimes wore a red jacket over the basic blue and white outfit. In real life, Jerry Cohan wore pince-nez eyeglasses, and if you want a touch of authenticity they are an option.

Actors playing multiple characters should make simple but distinctive costume changes or alterations so it is clear to the audience they are playing different characters. For example, it is recommended that the same middle-aged character actor play B. F. Keith, A. E. Erlanger, Julian Mitchell, the Reporter, Isidore Witmark, the burlesque comic, and assorted critics. In our original production the highly versatile actor playing these roles created unique characterizations by changing his posture, timbre, accent, way of phrasing: imaginative changes of hats, coats, ties, and glasses to create different looks helped reinforce the changes he made by his acting skills.

Playing director Julian Mitchell, for example, the actor wore a burgundy blazer draped over his shoulders—his arms were not in the sleeves—plus a gold silk ascot and pocket square. And he affected a bit of "attitude." As A. E. Erlanger, he wore a derby, rimless glasses, a vest and a dark jacket, and seemed a bit more down to earth. As B. F. Keith, he wore a different, "louder" looking jacket, and changed his body language to appear taller and more combative. As the doctor, the actor wore a bland, dark suit, conservative glasses, and carried a clipboard with papers. As the reporter, he wore a fedora tilted back on his head, with a loose tie around the unbuttoned collar of a nondescript shirt; he had no jacket, his shirt sleeves were rolled up. For his appearances as critics, he had two different pairs of jackets, and two different pairs of glasses. He made costume changes quickly (when appearing onstage as Keith, he actually was wearing two jackets, so that after playing Keith he could remove one jacket quickly to come onstage a moment later dressed as Erlanger).

But his skills as an actor counted for more than the costume changes—valuable though they were—for he made us believe just by voice, that he was different characters. For critic James Metcalfe, he spoke in a condescending, upper-class voice vaguely evocative of James Buckley; as Erlanger, he spoke with the engaging self-assurance of a vaudevillian delivering one-liners; as Keith, he seemed abrasive, quick to anger; as Mitchell, he spoke with a dash of theatricality. Having a variety of different period jackets, in distinctive colors and styles, and hats, and ties, and glasses, will help make it clear to the audience whether the actor is now Keith, Erlanger, Witmark, Mitchell, the Reporter, a Critic, a burlesque comic, or anyone else.

Similarly, another actor—young, handsome, a good singer—will double as the Male Singer, the Distraught Actor, Josh Brock, and Reporter #1. It should be clear from both costume and change of voice, posture, etc. that each is a distinct characterization. As the Male singer, performing "Forty-Five Minutes from Broadway" and singing the lead on "Sweet Popularity," he should wear an attractive period suit, including vest and tie. As Josh Brock, he might wear a stylish, flattering striped shirt—no vest or jacket—with an open collar. (He could consider parting his hair differently as well, looking sharp, but different from however he looks as The Male Singer.) As the distraught actor, a different
shirt and jacket is recommended; he can look a bit disheveled; his hair can be a bit out of place, his clothes can be a bit wrinkled or ill-fitting. When simply appearing in numbers as a member of the ensemble, he can wear a white shirt, no jacket, with perhaps vest and a tie.

The actor playing Percy, the Young Vaudevillian, the Young Actor, and Reporter #2, can subtly change his characterizations by wearing a period ticking cap as Percy and talking in an earnest, more naive way; by adopting something of a wiseguy manner as the Young Vaudevillian, wearing a colored or striped shirt, and carrying some cigarettes or a pouch of tobacco; perhaps wearing eyeglasses as the Young Actor, etc.

Sam Harris should wear businesslike trousers, vest, dress shirt, and tie.

The actress playing Faye Templeton can dress in the basic dark blue and white when just a member of the ensemble, but can wear something more stylish yet dignified (since she is supposed to be Broadway's reigning female star) for the scene in which she sings "Mary" and "Forty-Five Minutes from Broadway."

All performers should have character shoes in addition to their tap shoes. To whatever extent is possible, tap shoes should only be worn in scenes where the performers will actually be tapping. If performers try to wear tap shoes throughout the whole play, the tap shoes will create too much distracting noise as the performers walk about.

We chose in our original production to have ensemble members maintain one basic blue-and-white look throughout the production, and to give most principals a single costume. But if your budget permits and you're interested in experimenting, there are ample opportunities to try additional stylish period costumes in this show, perhaps adding life and color. If you would like to give, for example, "The American Rag Time"—the musical number which opens Act Two—a different look from anything seen earlier, that could be fun. The Four Cohans could have some costume variations, perhaps appearing a bit fancier in some scenes where they are supposed to be performing songs for an audience than in other scenes when they are simply talking. Cohan sometimes used a straw hat and cane in his stage appearances—another option to consider.

PROPS

A coatrack (which remains downstage right throughout the play). This can be wooden or metal, so long as it looks like It could have been used in Cohan's era. On the coatrack, from the start of the play, is a vintage overcoat (it could be a trench coat) and a fedora. A cane is there, too.

A folding screen. This is at stage left, in the opening scene of the play. Some red, white, and blue patriotic bunting is draped over it.

Three vaudeville-style placards (announcing which act is performing now) and a stand or easel to hold. These are preset, downstage right. At the start of the show, we see the top-most placard, which reads: "George M. Cohan and his Royal Family." This will be removed, at the point indicated in the script, to reveal the next placard, which reads: "The Four Cohans." This will be removed at a much later point (as indicated in the script) to reveal the final placard: "Mr. Cohan, Alone." The placards should be hand-lettered with a period feel, and should be large enough (20 inches wide and 30 inches high, or larger) to be readable by anyone in the audience.

Newspapers, to be carried by the members of the ensemble and by GMC in the musical number, "The Man Who Owns Broadway." The newspaper that GMC will use should be preset—placed on top of the piano for him to casually pick up just before doing the number. The copies for the other members of the ensemble should be stored until needed in the props area backstage. For the newspapers, select tabloid pages that do not have anything obviously anachronistic on them that the audience would notice. Pages with lots of indistinguishable text are ideal; a page with a big headline about President George Bush—or anything else that would be jarring in a scene supposedly occurring in the early 20th century—should be avoided.

Two bouquets of flowers, to be used in the "You Remind Me of My Mother" number.

Canes. You will need one cane, preset at the coatrack, which GMC will use near the close of the show. You will also need canes, stored the props area backstage, which Jerry Cohan will use when performing "Always Leave Them Laughing When You Say Goodbye," and which the burlesque comic will use in his scene. Canes were often used in vaudeville. If your choreographer chooses to have all Four Cohans use canes for one of their song-and-dance sequences (as our choreographer did in our original production), you will need canes for all Four Cohans. But having them all use canes for a song-and-dance routine is optional, depending on your choreographer's preferences.

Sheets of music (songs that GMC is supposed to have written). Some sheets should be preset on top of the piano. Some should be stored until needed in the props area backstage. GMC will show music that he has written (which he's been carrying around with him) to Isidore Witmark and to the Young Vaudevillian. Later, he will use sheets to help teach his family the song "I Want You." He'll also hand music to the pianist to play, when rehearsing "Harrigan" with Percy.

A pouch of tobacco, to be carried by the Young Vaudevillian who says he is "just going out for a smoke."

A rubber chicken, to be carried in one hand by the male burlesque comic. A big kettle, to be strapped to the back of the male burlesque comic. Rope, to be used both for tying the big kettle to the back of the comic, and also to suggest a leash (the comic is supposed to be walking a dog; we need not actually see the dog, so long as he is carrying a leash or a long piece of rope to imply a dog is trailing behind him).

An American flag that GMC can carry over his shoulder (the way a soldier might carry a rifle), in the "American Rag Time" number. This is optional. But if an American flag is used in this number, it should be the only American flag used in the play. Cohan's lyrics are so patriotic that there is no need to underline the message by filling the stage with flags; if you simply, sincerely, sing Cohan's lyrics to songs like "You're a Grand Old Flag" and "Over There," the audience will "see" the flags without your needing to physically have flags on stage. The play is intended to be evocative and impressionistic rather than literal. While it might seem tempting to give every member of the ensemble a flag to wave, the effect would be overkill. And if any member of the ensemble should accidentally drop a flag, the play's impact would be compromised.

A suicide note, carried by the distraught actor, who shows it to GMC.

The manuscript of a play, which Isidore Witmark carries and gives to GMC for evaluation.

Note pads, for reporters to carry.

A clipboard with paper on it, to be carried by GMC's doctor.

A suitcase, which Josie Cohan will carry when she tells GMC she is leaving the family act to marry Fred Niblo.

A chair—a simple black wooden chair will suffice—which director Julian Mitchell will sit on, and which GMC will use later in singing "Life's a Funny Proposition After All."

SOUND EFFECTS

The following sound effects are needed: the sound of a vintage telephone ringing (for a scene that is taking place in 1904), and the sound of a skyrocket going off. (If you do not have suitable sound-effect recordings, the pianist can improvise suitable sounds.)

LIGHTING SUGGESTIONS

Lighting needs are straightforward. You want to be able to isolate performers so that at times, for example, one speaker might be addressing the audience, fully lit, while everyone else stands still on stage in comparative darkness.

A strobe light will be needed, for when the skyrocket explodes. (GMC, in the script, is told to watch for the skyrocket. He looks out over the audience; we hear the skyrocket going off, and the strobe light goes off.)

You will need a follow spot (and a follow-spot operator), to keep Cohan in the spotlight as he dances or strides about the stage.

Stage lighting in Cohan's era tended to rely more on footlights than is common today; you can use footlights to help evoke a period feel.

For "Over There" we used yellow lighting to create a slightly surreal effect, since the number is taking place in the memory of a dying man.

SETS

For our original New York production, we did not have sets. Cohan's world was the theater, and we essentially used the theater itself as our set—a stage area defined by standard black curtains (plus two black rolling panels angled out a bit from the rear curtain). We also created a small alcove, downstage right, to give the piano, coatrack, and vaudeville placard some separation from the main performance area. You can create such an alcove if you wish (using curtains to do so), but that is not a necessity. If your theater has a proscenium arch or a wall that Cohan can touch, or do a turn off of, in a dance routine, it should be utilized; Cohan made use of every bit of the stage, including the proscenium arch.

We opted not to have a set primarily for artistic reasons. (The cost savings was a factor, too.) We wanted the show to have a slightly abstract, rather than literal, feel. We are seeing events as Cohan and others recall them. We wanted the show to move swiftly, in Cohan's tradition. And we did not want to pause for set changes.

But you can do as much or as little as you wish, in terms of creating sets for your production of this show. If you want a backdrop depicting a British racetrack for the "I'm a Yankee Doodle Dandy" number, or England's Southhampton Pier for "Give My Regards to Broadway," or if you want to bring a desk and chair onstage to suggest Witmark's office for the scene when Cohan meets Witmark, or if you want to have Cohan sing and dance atop a table for the scene in which he is honoring Josh Brock ... all of these are possibilities. You could use platforms to add variety to dance sequences. This show, featuring so many musical numbers, can be mounted effectively countless different ways.

POPULAR BIOGRAPHICAL MUSICALS AND REVUES

BACK TO BACHARACH AND DAVID
The Songs of Burt Bacharach and Hal David
Conceived by Steve Gunderson and Kathy Najimy

BY STROUSE
Music by Charles Strouse
Lyrics by Lee Adams, Martin Charmin, Fred Tobias,
David Rogers and Charles Strouse

COLE
A Entertainment Based on the Words and Music of Cole Porter
Devised by Benny Green and Alan Strachan

COWARDY CUSTARD
*A Musical Entertainment Featuring the
Words and Music of Noël Coward*
Devised by Gerald Frow, Alan Strachan and Wendy Toye

HOT 'N COLE
A Cole Porter Celebration!
Devised by David Armstrong, Mark Waldrop and
Bruce W. Coyle with Musical Arrangements by Bruce W. Coyle

JERRY'S GIRLS
*A Broadway Entertainment
The Music and Lyrics of Jerry Herman*
Concept by Larry Alfrod, Wayne Cilento and Jerry Herman

JOLSON AND COMPANY
By Stephen Mo Hannan and Jay Berkow

JOYFUL NOISE
(The Story Behind Handel's "The Messiah")
A Play with Music by Tim Slover

LADY DAY AT EMERSON'S BAR & GRILL
By Lanie Robertson

POPULAR MUSICALS from Samuel French

After the Ball
Avenue X
The Best Little Whorehouse in Texas
The Big Bang
Blood Brothers
Chess
Chicago
Clue: The Musical
Das Barbecü
Eating Raoul
Do Patent Leather Shoes Really Reflect Up?
Doctor! Doctor!
Evelyn and the Polka King
The Gig
Grease
The Green Heart
Gunmetal Blues
The It Girl
It Ain't Nothing But the Blues
James A. Michener's Sayonora
James Joyce's The Dead
Kiss of the Spider Woman
La Cage aux Folles
The Last Session
Leader of the Pack: The Ellie Greenwich Musical
Little Mary Sunshine
Mack & Mabel
Me and My Girl
A New Brain
New York Rock

AVAILABLE FOR MANY SAMUEL FRENCH MUSICALS
Original Cast Recordings on CD
Demo Tapes
Promotional Posters

POPULAR MUSICALS
from Samuel French

୶ଡ଼୶ଡ଼୶ଡ଼୶ଡ଼

The 1940's Radio Hour
No Way to Treat a Lady
Noël and Gertie
Nunsence / Nunsense A-Men!
Opal
Pageant
Pete 'n' Keely
Peter Pan
Phantom
Pippi Longstocking: The Family Musical
Pump Boys and Dinettes
Radio Gals
Return to the Forbidden Planet
Richard O'Brien's The Rocky Horror Show
Ruthless!
Sail Away
Sander's Family Christmas
Scrooge!
The Secret Garden
Shenadoah
Side Show
Smoke on the Mountain
Song of Singapore
The Spitfire Grill
Starmites
Steel Pier
Sweet & Hot: The Songs of Harold Arlen
Swingtime Canteen
They're Playing Our Song
The Wiz
Zombie Prom

**AVAILABLE FOR MANY
SAMUEL FRENCH MUSICALS**
Original Cast Recordings on CD
Demo Tapes
Promotional Posters

PS3604.E444 G46 2004x
Deffaa, Chip, 1951-
George M. Cohan in his own words